"AND YOU WILL KNOW

THE TRUTH AND THE TRUTH

WILL SET YOU FREE."

JOHN 8:32

INTRODUCTION

Life as you know it may never be the same. No matter where you are in your faith journey, this curriculum will challenge you to take a step toward truth—about God, about faith, and about yourself.

It is for freedom that Christ set us free. That's what Paul wrote in Galatians 5:1, and Jesus Himself said that He came to the earth so that we may have life and have it to the full (John 10:10). Just imagine that: Life abundant. Not barely surviving, but truly living. It means days filled with hope, joy, and purpose. This is the kind of life God always intended for you to have.

God wants a relationship with you, and He sent his son, Jesus, to bridge the gap between earth and heaven so you could know Him. The journey may not be easy, but it will be rewarding. During this semester, you will be the one who decides how far you are willing to go to find freedom. Here is a promise from Jeremiah 29:13: If you seek Him with your whole heart, you will find Him.

The pursuit of *Freedom* begins today.

TABLE OF CONTENTS

1	**Week One** – Video Notes: The Tree of Life
7	**Week Two** – The Tree of the Knowledge of Good and Evil
25	**Week Three** – The Tree of Life
39	**Week Four** – Spiritual Order
59	**Week Five** – Video Notes: Overflow of the Heart
65	**Week Six** – A Life of Surrender
77	**Week Seven** – Forgiveness
103	**Week Eight** – The Power of Words
123	**Week Nine** – The Living Word
139	**Week Ten** – Video Notes: Vessels of Honor
145	**Week Eleven** – Vessels of Honor
165	**Week Twelve** – Worship
185	**Appendix**
186	Preparing for the Conference
189	Freedom Song: Scriptures for Living in Freedom
212	The Armor of God
214	Who I Am in Christ
217	Answer Key

Note: Unless otherwise noted, all Scriptures are taken from the New Living Translation (NLT). Other translations used in these materials are New King James Version (NKJV), New International Version (NIV), The Amplified Bible (AMP), New American Standard Bible (NASB), and the Message Bible (MSG).

Second Edition – V4 – July 2019

SECTION ONE

THE TREE OF LIFE

WEEK ONE
THE TREE OF LIFE

"Now the Lord God had planted a garden in the east, in Eden; and there He put the man He had formed. And the Lord God made all kinds of trees grow out of the ground—trees that were pleasing to the eye and good for food. In the middle of the garden were the tree of life and the tree of the knowledge of good and evil... And the Lord God commanded the man, 'You are free to eat from any tree in the garden; but you must not eat from the tree of the knowledge of good and evil, for when you eat from it you will certainly die.'"

GENESIS 2:8–9, 16–17 NIV

THE CHOICE

The Tree of the Knowledge of Good and Evil Says:
_____ to get to God.
The Tree of Life says:
Receive the fact that Jesus has already _____.

> *You study the Scriptures diligently because you think that in them you have eternal life. These are the very Scriptures that testify about me, yet you refuse to come to me to have life.*
> JOHN 5:39-40 NIV

The Tree of the Knowledge of Good and Evil says:
Keep trying to get _____.
The Tree of Life says:
Receive the fact that He _____.

> *But God demonstrates his own love for us in this: While we were still sinners, Christ died for us.*
> ROMANS 5:8 NIV

The Tree of the Knowledge of Good and Evil says: _____
The Tree of Life says: _____

> *This is love for God: to obey His commands. And His commands are not burdensome. Whoever has the Son has life; whoever does not have the Son of God does not have life.*
> 1 JOHN 5:3,12 NIV

FOUR RESPONSES

1. Fall in love _____.

   If you love me, you will obey what I command.
   JOHN 14:15 NIV

2. Serve God through _____ not _____.

   "Do not think that I have come to abolish the Law or the Prophets. I have not come to abolish them but to fulfill them."
   MATTHEW 5:17 NIV

3. Respond to all sin with _____.

   Therefore, there is now no condemnation for those who are in Christ Jesus.
   ROMANS 8:1 NIV

4. Guard your _____ from going back.

What am I going to do to be Godly?

This day I call the heavens and the earth as witnesses against you that I have set before you life and death, blessings and curses. Now choose life, so that you and your children may live.
DEUTERONOMY 30:19 NIV

Journal

WEEK TWO

THE TREE OF THE KNOWLEDGE OF GOOD AND EVIL

"But the Lord God warned him, "You may freely eat the fruit of every tree in the garden—except the Tree of the Knowledge of Good and Evil. If you eat its fruit, you are sure to die."

GENESIS 2:16-17

The Tree of Life is more than just a backdrop to a Bible story; it can be a way of life. To find out how, let's start at the beginning: Genesis, the first book of the Bible. In Chapter 1, the first Scriptures tell us about the creation of our world and define God as the Creator and Ruler who has authority and dominion. The second story in the Bible tells us about Adam and Eve, the first sin, and the two trees in the Garden of Eden.

It's the second story for a reason: Everything else in the Bible hinges on it. From it we learn humanity has to choose every day between the Tree of Life and the Tree of the Knowledge of Good and Evil.

> **Tree of Life**
> Freedom, Grace, Eternal life, God is good, God is forgiving
> **Tree of the Knowledge of Good and Evil**
> Bondage, The Law, Leads to death, God is only a judge, We are condemned

When we study Scripture, it's always a good idea to find the first place a subject is mentioned. In our journey to walk in communion with God in freedom, we must find out why we may be separated from God and why we may be in bondage. The first place in the Bible where separation from God is mentioned is Genesis 3. The first people God created made a bad choice that caused this separation. (See Romans 5:12)

Prior to Genesis 3, Adam and Eve walked with God and enjoyed His presence. The Word tells us God made these two humans in His image and gave Adam dominion over everything He had created. God gave Adam authority through the relationship that He established with him. Without their relationship, Adam would not have had authority. When Adam and Eve sinned, they forfeited this authority.

Through deception and rebellion, the serpent took the authority and dominion that God had given to man. The Bible tells us that satan's desire was to exalt his throne above the stars of God. (Isaiah 14:13) Until the fall of man, he lacked power and influence to set up rulership. Jesus called satan "the ruler of this world." (John 12:31)

TRUTHS ABOUT THE FRUIT OF THE TREE OF THE KNOWLEDGE OF GOOD AND EVIL

1. The fruit is knowledge.

Most of us think of this fruit as some sort of apple, but it's not. The fruit of this tree is exactly what the Bible says: knowledge (information, data, ideas, worldview, thought patterns)—the knowledge of good and evil. God was basically saying to Adam and Eve, "If you change your way of thinking, it will create separation between us. If you change your worldview, you won't be able to understand Me and relate to Me." Satan says, "It won't hurt you to think like that."

Note that God didn't say it's wrong to have knowledge. In fact, God said to Israel through Hosea the prophet, "My people are destroyed for lack of knowledge."(Hosea 4:6 NKJV) The issue isn't necessarily knowledge; rather, it's the motive behind its acquisition. In other words, why do we desire knowledge? Is it to gain God's wisdom and understanding, or is it to somehow exalt ourselves?

> *We know that "We all possess knowledge." But knowledge puffs up while love builds up.*
> 1 CORINTHIANS 8:1 NIV

According to Colossians 2:3, what do we find hidden in Jesus?

....

....

From the beginning, human beings have desired to be wise. God is actually pleased with this desire. In 1 Kings, we have the account of God appearing to King Solomon in a dream and saying to him, "What do you want? Ask, and I will give it to you!" Solomon asked for one thing: wisdom to govern the nation of Israel and the ability to discern good from evil.

Read 1 Kings 3:10-13. How did God respond to Solomon's request?

....

....

Wisdom from God varies greatly from wisdom from the world. We can tell the difference between the two by observing characteristics of each.

Wisdom from God:
Pure, peace-loving, gentle at all times, willing to yield to others, full of mercy and good deeds, showing no partiality, always sincere
Wisdom from the world:
Jealous, selfish, earthly, unspiritual, motivated by evil

When do we need wisdom? All the time! We are constantly making decisions, and even the smallest ones can be made with wisdom from God. Using godly wisdom allows us to become more like God as we emulate Him. His wisdom draws us closer to Himself. Worldly wisdom leads us to sin, which alienates us from God. James 1:5 says, "If you need wisdom, ask our generous God, and He will give it to you. He will not rebuke you for asking"

2. The fruit is deadly.

> *The Lord God warned him, "You may freely eat the fruit of every tree in the garden—except the Tree of the Knowledge of Good and Evil. If you eat its fruit, you are sure to die."*
> **GENESIS 2:16-17**

Eating from the Tree of Knowledge (consuming knowledge) in your own pursuit of godliness is deadly. Satan didn't tempt Eve with blatant rebellion. He said, "Go ahead and eat this fruit. It will make you like God." Satan tempted Eve with her desire to become like God. It's important to note that often the desire to know is in direct opposition to the desire to trust. We would rather gain knowledge to try to control our own lives than trust God to take care of us.

Read Genesis 3:22-24. Why were Adam and Eve driven from the Garden of Eden?
....

....

Adam and Eve didn't die physically when they ate from the Tree of Knowledge; they died spiritually. Through Adam's disobedience, death entered the entire human race, and we are all born spiritually dead in need of resurrection. The good news is that, through Jesus, we have access to the Tree of Life. If we pursue Life Himself in our desire for godliness, we will become truly like Him.

3. The fruit is consumed.

> *"The woman was convinced. She saw that the tree was beautiful and its fruit looked delicious, and she wanted the wisdom it would give her. So she took some of the fruit and ate it. Then she gave some to her husband, who was with her, and he ate it, too."*
> **GENESIS 3:6**

"Eating" is not just putting food in your mouth. It literally means to "consume" or "ingest." Ideas are ingested in our minds and then sin is conceived. How did the first sin come about? Eve talked to Adam about it. Through a conversation, they consumed the idea and began to process it. This progression tells us that sin does not begin with the act, it begins in our minds.

We have to be very careful about the things we ingest because they can have a lasting effect on our lives. For instance, watching certain movies or television shows might expose you to images that could trouble you for the rest of your life. Likewise, spending time reading and studying certain types of ideologies has the potential to pollute your mind and lead you to ruin and despair. Just as a parent takes extra care to guide what their children are exposed to, we should take the same caution with what we let ourselves be exposed to.

4. The fruit causes separation.

> *"The man and his wife hid themselves from the presence of the Lord God among the trees of the garden."*
> **GENESIS 3:8 NASB**

Again, remember that it was man who hid from God. Many have been taught that Adam and Eve sinned and that God, in His holiness and His righteousness, turned His back on Adam and Eve because His holiness could not stand to be in the presence of sinful man. But that's not what the Bible says. The Bible says Adam and Eve sinned, their eyes were opened, they covered up, and then they hid from God because they were ashamed and afraid of His reaction. The truth is, Adam and Eve misjudged how God would respond to their sin. He wasn't watching from behind a tree, waiting for them to fail so He could judge them. God searched for them as He walked through the garden, calling out, "Where are you?" because He loved them. God is not watching and waiting in anticipation for us to fall short. God is love (1 John 4:8) and the Bible says that "love covers a multitude of sins." (1 Peter 4:8) When we see His heart for us, we will run to Him instead of hiding from Him when we sin.

From Romans 8:38-39, name all the things that cannot separate us from the love of God.

....

....

THE TREE OF THE KNOWLEDGE OF GOOD AND EVIL PRODUCES SHAME AND VICTIMIZATION

> *"[Adam] replied, 'I heard you walking in the garden, so I hid. I was afraid because I was naked.' 'Who told you that you were naked?' the Lord God asked. 'Have you eaten from the tree whose fruit I commanded you not to eat?' The man replied, 'It was the woman you gave me who gave me the fruit, and I ate it.' Then the Lord God asked the woman, 'What have you done?' 'The serpent deceived me,' she replied. 'That's why I ate it.'"*
> **GENESIS 3:10–13**

The Tree of the Knowledge of Good and Evil robs us of innocence.

Imagine this situation to see how this process might happen: a young teenage boy has always been a delight to his parents—bright-eyed, enthusiastic, and curious, with no hesitation about him. But his mother begins to notice a change in him. He is becoming serious and angry, coming home with droopy shoulders and his head hung. The sparkle has left his eyes. He barely speaks to his parents and goes straight to his room. One day, while picking up laundry off his bedroom floor, his mother notices pornographic magazines under his bed. She begins to understand what has happened: Her bright, lively son now has darkness inside of him. His innocence has been polluted; he is no longer a little boy. Knowledge of the evil in those magazines advanced the kingdom of darkness in his life. All the things he saw in the magazines were real and true—the issue is, he didn't need to know. Now that he has allowed that darkness inside of him, he is filled with shame, and he isn't able to relate to his parents like he used to. It's not that his parents have distanced themselves from him; his sin has caused him to pull away from them in shame. He is no longer innocent.

Shame causes us to separate ourselves from God, making it so that we cannot operate in the freedom that Christ has for us. Shame is a veil that comes between God and us. It covers us completely, even our eyes, so that we can see only dimly who and where God is. God said to Adam and Eve, "Who told you that you were naked?" His tone was probably like that of the teenage boy's mother, filled with great sadness and angst. "Who gave you those magazines? You really shouldn't know that." God doesn't want us to eat from the Tree of the Knowledge of Good and Evil because it builds barriers—like shame—between Him and us. Those barriers break His heart. He wants to be close to us.

Shame causes us to do all sorts of things that keep us from connecting with God. Shame makes us want to hide. Prior to eating the forbidden fruit, Adam and Eve were both naked and were not ashamed (Genesis 2:25). Afterwards, they came up with the idea of sewing fig leaves together to cover themselves and then tried to hide from God's presence in the trees of the garden.

The Results of Shame

1. Covering up with religion and becoming focused on works
2. Lying, deception, false pride
3. Making promises we can't keep
4. Getting our self-worth from the things that we do
5. Inability to come to a place of honesty with God because we believe we have no true value
6. Concentrating on our sin instead of concentrating on our Savior

Why is shame so deadly? Because it strips us of the power to change. It keeps us from receiving the provision God made for our sin through the blood of Jesus. There is a difference between guilt and shame. Guilt is about what we have done, but shame is about who we are. With guilt, we can always get a fresh start. With shame, we are caught in a noose because the problem stays with us. In fact, with shame, we are the problem. In order to be free from shame, we must begin to see ourselves as God sees us.

Ask yourself: *Have you ever been overcome by shame?*
What steps can you take to remove the barrier of shame from your life?

Just as the Tree of the Knowledge of Good and Evil produces shame in our lives, it also makes us susceptible to victimization. Victimization is a natural response to our sin. Eve responded, "The devil made me do it." and Adam responded, "The woman you gave me made me do it." We blame others, displacing responsibility. When we place blame, we excuse our internal condition or difficult outward circumstances by focusing on the actions of others. We say, "If my husband would just treat me right, I wouldn't be so unhappy and manipulative." "If my family were less argumentative, I wouldn't be so irritable." "If everybody would just live like they are supposed to, everything would work right."

The Results of Victimization

1. We notice others' sins, but not our own.
2. We excuse and condemn ourselves, saying, "I've just always been this way. I'll never change. I'll never be good enough."
3. We feel rejected.

Whether we victimize ourselves by blaming others or excusing and condemning ourselves, we are powerless to change. This is why victimization is so deadly.

Are there any areas of your life—perhaps with your parents or other people in your past, in your marriage, at work, with friends, or even at church—where you have taken on a "victim mentality"? How should you change your way of thinking regarding that situation?

With victimization and shame, we're either the Pharisee or the woman caught in adultery (John 8). We're either saying, "You're not good enough," or, "I'm not good enough"—basing our relationships with

God and others on behavior and merit, but that's not the perspective God wants us to have. That's Tree of the Knowledge of Good and Evil thinking, and it keeps us from changing and connecting with God. It's a trap of the enemy devised to keep us from changing. The devil wants us to be forever stuck in the world of blame and self-condemnation.

We must get to a point where, no matter what happens, we take responsibility for our own lives. We can no longer blame anyone else for the quality of our relationship with God.

The fruit of the Tree of the Knowledge of Good and Evil lacks the power to transform the heart. It can provide facts and information, but it is powerless to give you life.

> *"Jesus spoke to the people once more and said, I am the light of the world. If you follow Me, you won't have to walk in the darkness, because you will have the light that leads to life."'*
> JOHN 8:12

Journal

WEEK THREE
THE TREE OF LIFE

"For you have been called to live in freedom, my brothers and sisters."
GALATIANS 5:13

Last week, we studied the two trees in the Garden of Eden and how they each represented a way of living. We explored how the Tree of the Knowledge of Good and Evil and its deadly fruit led to shame and victimization. This week, we will look at the Tree of Life and its ability to set us free from incorrect thoughts about God and ourselves.

If you have weak muscles that you haven't been using correctly, you might begin a weight-training program to grow in strength and skill. As followers of Jesus, we have to build up our faith by reading God's Word, retraining our thought processes to line up with Biblical truth. Just like weight lifters need a spotter to help encourage, challenge, and assist them when the burden is heavy, we need partnership and support in this faith-building process. This Small Group is designed for your leaders and fellow group members to help you learn how to truly live in freedom.

As you progress through this group, you will be able to use Tree of Life thinking as a framework for the way you approach every situation you encounter. Remember that God's commands were never meant to be burdensome. In fact, as you grow close to Him and learn to hear His voice, you will find His heart for you. His divine plan was made for your sake—not for His. He simply wants to protect you from very real danger, and He desires your success.

Write *Zephaniah 3:17.*

THE FRUIT OF LIVING IN THE TREE OF LIFE

1. The Tree of Life results in fellowship with God.

> *"Now this is eternal life: that they know You, the only true God, and Jesus Christ, whom you have sent."*
> JOHN 17:3 NIV

According to Vine's Bible Dictionary, "know" in this verse is the Greek word *ginosko*, which means to recognize, to understand, or to understand completely. It indicates a relationship. The only way to experience abundant life is by truly knowing the living God. He asked us to love Him, but only after His lavish display of love for us through the sacrifice of Jesus. "God showed how much He loved us by sending His one and only Son into the world so that we might have eternal life through Him. This is real love—not that we loved God, but that He loved us and sent his Son as a sacrifice to take away our sins." (1 John 4:9–10) The Bible says in 1 John 4:19 that the only reason we have any love at all is because He first loved us.

God loved us so much that He sent His Son to die on a cross to make a way for us to be in relationship with Him. The cross represents more than a sacrificial death. It is a promise, a blood covenant, God made with His Son so that we could have confidence that He would never change His mind about His relationship with us (Hebrews 6:17–18). In the Old Testament, God made covenants with man, and man always broke them. This time, God sealed the covenant with the blood of His Son Jesus so that nothing can separate us from His love.

2. Fellowship with God results in innocence—not the other way around.

"They realized they were naked." (Genesis 3:7 NIV) As we spend time walking with God, listening to His voice, talking to Him, obeying Him, worshipping Him, and enjoying Him, we will notice a transformation taking place, not only on the outside, but on the inside as well. We will become, in a sense, "naked" or transparent and unashamed before Him.

"Nakedness," in Genesis 3:7, speaks of innocence. Adam and Eve were unaware of any reason to hide anything from God. They had no sin-consciousness. Think of little kids running around with no clothes on after a bath. Absolutely no shame! Childlike innocence is an amazing virtue. Adam and Eve's nakedness was part of the innocence and simplicity of their lives. Before they sinned, they had nothing to be ashamed of. This is the same concept Jesus was talking about when He said we had to be like little children to enter the Kingdom of Heaven (Matthew 19:14). Children are not technically innocent; they just don't have any hesitation about them. They are not weighed down by guilt, shame, or burdens.

1 Corinthians 14:20 (NIV) says, "Brothers and sisters, stop thinking like children. In regard to evil be infants, but in your thinking be adults." God wants us to be mature in our thinking, but for the Kingdom of God to work powerfully in you, you must foster a childlike spirit. Childlikeness may look to some like naivety or simple-mindedness, but it is actually a Biblical way to live. Jesus says we should be as shrewd as a snake and as innocent as a dove. (Matthew 10:16) That's a mysterious and rare combination for the world we live in! Paul says in 1 Corinthians 1:27 that "God deliberately chose things the world considers foolish in order to shame those who think they are wise." Dare to be misunderstood

in your pursuit of relationship with God because only the pure in heart will see Him.

Simple innocence is born out of a friendship with God. It happens when we rest in God. We abide in His favor and presence so that when someone offends us, we can respond with kindness instead of anger. As we are transformed into the image of God, we become less and less affected by the negativity of the world. If we truly live with an innocent spirit, the enemy has no ammunition. If we sin, we know how to receive forgiveness, and if someone offends us, we know how to forgive.

Read Matthew 5:39-44 and Luke 6:27-36. In these passages, Jesus tells us how to live as a child of God in innocence and freedom. Using the Scriptures as a reference, describe what living in innocence looks like.

....

....

3. Innocence is a conduit of God's power.

"The Spirit of the Lord is on me, because He has anointed me to proclaim good news to the poor. He has sent me to proclaim freedom for the prisoners and recovery of sight for the blind, to set the oppressed free, to proclaim the year of the Lord's favor." (Luke 4:18-19 NIV) This is what Jesus said after His great temptation by satan in the desert. He came out full of the Holy Spirit and power to begin His public ministry. This Scripture says God anointed Jesus to preach good news. What does it mean to be "anointed" to do something? It means to be empowered by the Holy Spirit. When we are filled with the Holy Spirit and abide in Jesus, we become free from the works of darkness in our lives. We become vessels of honor useful to God. Innocence keeps our minds and hearts pure, helping us continually recognize our need for God. An attitude of dependence on God is fertile ground for the anointing of the Holy Spirit. As we seek God and submit our lives to Him, He equips us for every good work (2 Timothy 3:17).

Rewrite Acts 10:38, replacing Jesus' name with your name and "Nazareth" with the name of your city. Read it out loud.

....

....

Jesus said in John 15:5 (NIV), "I am the vine; you are the branches. If you remain in me and I in you, you will bear much fruit; apart from me you can do nothing." Innocence and power always produce the gifts and fruit of the Holy Spirit.

4. Innocence results in freedom.

"It is for freedom that Christ has set us free." (Galatians 5:1 NIV) This is the mystery of godliness: we will sin and fall, but if we sin with the Tree of Life as our perspective, we can easily receive forgiveness and get back up. How quickly we get back up depends on the degree of understanding we have in our hearts of the completeness of God's forgiveness.

What does Psalm 37:23-24 say happens when the Godly stumble?

....

....

When we approach life with an innocent spirit, it changes the way we live and think about every part of our lives. If we attend church in the Tree of Life, we will love everything about it. We will love the pastor, the people, and the worship, because we are focused on the Reason we go to church in the first place. On the other hand, thinking in terms of the Tree of the Knowledge of Good and Evil will result in ideas like, "These songs are too long and too loud," "The preaching is too simple," "The children are too noisy," or "No one talked to me." Approaching life with innocence allows us to see the good things in front of us instead of picking every person, church, or situation apart. Innocence sets us free!

Relationships change in the innocence of the Tree of Life. We no longer hold people to impossible standards; we are quick to extend forgiveness and slow to take offense. Instead of looking for people to meet our needs, we look for ways to serve others. Because we live for Jesus and His Kingdom, people are no longer able to "take advantage" of us. This is true freedom.

Reading the Bible, praying, and serving others should be sources of life, security, strength, and delight to us. These things should never be religious duties that must be checked off a to-do list. In the innocence of the Tree of Life, we realize these tasks are done out of relationship, not responsibility. Falling in love with Jesus turns the idea of duty into devotion, and it is a beautiful and wonderful thing. Prayer will be powerful and reading the Bible will refresh our spirits when we're living in the Tree of Life. No more guilt-ridden sittings where we plow through twenty chapters a day because "that's what Christians do." Religion says, "Do it or suffer!" Relationship says, "Do it and live!"

Ask yourself: Do I feel completely innocent before God? What would it be like to have true fellowship with God?

"So now there is no condemnation for those who belong to Christ Jesus. And because you belong to Him, the power of the life-giving Spirit has freed you from the power of sin that leads to death."
ROMANS 8:1-2

HOW TO LIVE IN THE TREE OF LIFE

Now that we know it is possible to be free from bondage in our thinking, our actions, and our relationships with God and people, let's take a look at some powerful truths that can help us form a firm foundation upon which we can build a life that is both abundant and free. In order to move out of the shadow of the Tree of the Knowledge of Good and Evil and into the light of Tree of Life living, we must know who Jesus is and who we are because of Him. To help us understand this, we need to "be transformed by the renewing of [our minds]." Romans 12:1–3 (NIV)

Let's take a look at a few truths that will help us live in the Tree of Life.

We must remember that relationship with the Father is essential to living in the Tree of Life. In order to enjoy this right relationship with God, we must receive His extravagant love for us. Romans 5:8 (NIV) says that God expressed His great love for us in this way: "While we were still sinners, Christ died for us." Before we looked for God, He made a way for us to be in relationship with Him. He made the first move.

Because of the finished work of the cross, we are declared righteous before God. Romans 5:1 says: "Therefore, since we have been justified through faith, we have peace with God through our Lord Jesus Christ." Many of us have been serving God out of duty or fear—much like a servant. A servant has an obligation to do what is expected. He is required to be faithful or suffer consequences. A son serves because he is a part of the family. A son is faithful because of the love that he has for his father. Because of the sacrifice of Jesus, God now sees us as sons and daughters.

Read *Galatians 4:7 and 2 Corinthians 6:18. What does God say about your identity?*

....

....

Ask yourself: *Do I live my life as a son or as a servant?*

....

....

Recognize the two environments where you can live: the Tree of Life or the Tree of the Knowledge of Good and Evil. Knowing that you can choose a Tree of Life response and attitude in every circumstance is crucial to walking in freedom. It is a daily choice to respond with life and Godliness. Throughout the Bible, God compares the fruit of Godly decisions with the fruit of ungodly decisions. It is clearly God's desire that we live a life that produces Godly fruit. We can only do this by choosing to live God's way: in the Tree of Life.

In Matthew 11, Jesus compares His way of living to that of religious Pharisees. The Pharisees were legalistic and self-righteous. Their approach to God was in the strict keeping of all Jewish laws.

Read Matthew 11:28-30, and write out Jesus' response to the heavy burden that comes from trying to keep the law.

Read Deuteronomy 30:19 (NIV). Moses challenged the Israelites to determine what path they would follow. One path led to life, and the other led to death. He exhorted them, "Now choose life, so that you and your children may live."

Ask the Lord to help you to make life-giving decisions every day. Throughout the day, when faced with a difficult decision or situation, pause, examine your motives, and ask Him for wisdom. Though retraining the way we think and respond takes time, we learn and grow in both our successes and our failures. Remember God loves you, and He is for you. Grace was His idea.

Ask yourself: Do my daily responses and decisions bring life to others? In what tree do I live?

Renew your mind with what the Word of God says is true. Transformation can take place when we know what the Word of God says about our lives. Often, our worldview and past experiences shape our version of truth. We cannot make the Bible line up with what we think is true, but we can decide to align our beliefs with the truth of the Bible. In order to do this, we must consume the Word. Changing our internal truth will change our external responses.

Romans 12:2 (NIV) says, "Do not conform to the pattern of this world, but be transformed by the renewing of your mind. Then you will be able to test and approve what God's will is—His good, pleasing, and perfect will." The pattern of this world will lead to death. God's will leads to life.

2 Corinthians 10:5 says that every thought should be examined for Godly accuracy. If it does not line up with what the Bible says, we must take it captive and make it obedient to the Word of God. This will become a way of life as we practice putting God's Word ahead of our feelings and beliefs. In other words, don't just read the Bible, let it read you.

In Ephesians 4, Paul tells us to let the Holy Spirit renew our thoughts and our attitudes and to put on our new self that has been created in the very likeness of God in righteousness and holiness. These are choices we must intentionally make. We must choose to renew our thoughts, attitudes, and beliefs in God's Word, and we must choose to put on holiness and righteousness. If we do, we will begin to experience true Tree of Life living!

Read Philippians 4:8 and write out a way to renew your mind.

....

Journal

WEEK FOUR
SPIRITUAL ORDER

*"Now may the God of peace make you holy in every way,
and may your whole spirit and soul and body be kept blameless
until our Lord Jesus Christ comes again."*

1 THESSALONIANS 5:23

To daily live in the Tree of Life, you need to know two things: God designed you with three distinct parts, and you need to embrace the principles of spiritual order. Understanding spiritual order will help us get rid of the sin in our lives and walk in holiness and freedom. As believers, we long to live lives of fellowship with God. But while this is our desire, life in fellowship with God does not come naturally for us. Since the fall in the garden, mankind has battled a sin nature that wars against our desire to be holy. The Apostle Paul said that there is an internal struggle that goes on between the desire to do right and the natural tendency to do wrong.

Write Romans 7:21-23

....

....

God created us with three distinct parts:

1. A spirit that must be redeemed
2. A soul that must be restored
3. A body that must surrender

At the moment of salvation, our spirit is made alive in Christ and immediately put into right standing with God (Romans 3:24, 5:1). The Bible calls this event justification: "just-as-if I had never sinned." However, the soul and body will require time and effort to be conformed to the image of Christ (Ephesians 4:12–13). This gradual process is called sanctification.

God desires for us to be transformed into His image with ever-increasing glory. We must learn to hear His voice and be led by His spirit.

Write 2 Corinthians 3:16–18

"But whenever a person turns to the Lord, the veil is removed. Now the Lord is the Spirit, and where the Spirit of the Lord is, there is freedom. All of us, gazing with unveiled face on the glory of the Lord, are being transformed into the same image from glory to glory, as from the Lord who is the Spirit."

In Galatians 4:19, Paul portrays sanctification as a process. How long this process takes depends on our willingness to engage with the Word of God, accept it as absolute truth in our lives, and apply it to all of our circumstances.

THE SPIRIT

Did you know that you are a spiritual being having a temporary physical experience on earth rather than a physical being having a temporary spiritual experience? God's plan is that our spirits become the strongest part of our three-part design and be the "command center" of who we are and what we do.

> *"When you were dead in your sins and in the uncircumcision of your flesh, God made you alive with Christ. He forgave us all our sins, having canceled the charge of our legal indebtedness, which stood against us and condemned us; He has taken it away, nailing it to the cross."*
> **COLOSSIANS 2:13-14 NIV**

The blood of Jesus has forever purchased our capacity for friendship with God. This was the price God paid so that we could be reconciled back to Him and have the fellowship that Adam once enjoyed (2 Corinthians 5:18). The moment we are saved, we are made alive in Christ, forever redeemed and made righteous before the Father. Along with the gift of eternal life, we receive the Holy Spirit and immediately have the ability to be in relationship with God. In short, the cross of Christ bridges the chasm of death and gives us a way to have fellowship, communication, and access to the Tree of Life.

Just as a bride and groom are united in matrimony and become one, at the point of salvation, your spirit and the Spirit of Christ are united and become one.

Write *1 Corinthians 6:17*

....

....

Ask yourself: *How does knowing that my spirit is redeemed and in right standing with the Father change the way I see myself?*

....

....

Now that we are one with Christ, we have the ability to understand spiritual truth and discern right from wrong. We can adjust our lives to hear the voice of God. It is much like tuning a dial to pick up a radio station. Sometimes there may be static in the airwaves (distraction, confusion, fear, etc.), but if we continue to seek the Lord and His way of doing things, our spirit will rise above the static, and we will be able to tune in to the broadcast of truth.

Read *1 Corinthians 2:14, and write why the world cannot accept the things that come from God.*

....

....

THE SOUL

The soul is one of God's most beautiful creations. It enables us to experience relationships and appreciate the beauty of our surroundings. We have been made in the image of God with the capacity to think, reason, and express emotions. God could have programmed us to do and be whatever He wanted, but instead He gave us the ability to choose.

Our souls are made up of three parts:

1. The mind, which thinks and reasons
2. The will, which makes choices
3. The emotions, which believe, feel, and remember

Write out the verses below and identify
which of the three parts of the soul they address.

Proverbs 2:10

....

....

Psalm 119:167

....

....

Psalm 139:14

....

....

Write *Joshua 24:15*

....

Ask yourself: *Are my thoughts driven by emotion?*

....

THE BODY

In Genesis 2:7, we learn that God formed our bodies from the earth. The body acts as a temporary house or shell that contains our soul and spirit. 1 Corinthians 6:19 says that our bodies are the temple of the Holy Spirit. In the Old Testament, the presence of God was housed in the inner sanctuary of the temple called the Holy of Holies. At the death of Jesus, the veil of the temple was torn and the presence of God moved out of the structure and into the hearts of all believers. Just as we would not go to church and shatter the windows and destroy the furniture, we should not do anything to intentionally harm our bodies; they are special, designed by God, and given to us in order to carry out the plans He has for us on this earth.

Our bodies have appetites, both good and bad. The Bible says to be careful of any sin that leads to our flesh getting anything it wants. Often people want to know how far they can sin and still enjoy the benefits of God's blessing. The snare with sin is that it never satisfies. We are constantly looking to fulfill the next craving. Carnal desires cause us to need satisfaction, and though we may satisfy them in the moment, the craving soon returns and brings with it increased intensity. This cycle will repeat itself time and again until we break it by the power of the Holy Spirit.

Ask yourself: Are my actions driven by my cravings?

Read 1 Corinthians 6:12 (NIV), and fill in the blanks:

*"I have the right to do anything," you say—
but not everything is _____.
'I have the right to do anything'—
but I _____."*

Another real consequence of sin is the ripple effect. A filter for sinful actions should be: How will this action affect those around me? We should rehearse daily the consequences of sins and how they would affect our spouses, our family and our friends. Would your actions cause another to stumble or be offended?

Read 1 Corinthians 8:9 from The Message Bible and hear the heart of our Father:

> *"But God does care when you use your freedom carelessly in a way that leads a fellow believer still vulnerable to those old associations to be thrown off track."*
> 1 CORINTHIANS 8:9 MSG

ORDERED LIVING

Spiritual order provides a framework for living in the Tree of Life. It allows you to live with your spirit united with God, and your soul and body submitted to your spirit. In other words, your spirit, which is now one with God, calls the shots, and the soul and body follow. So here's the real question: If I am saved, why do I struggle with sin? The answer is found in the process of sanctification and the principle of spiritual order. When we give our lives to Jesus, we receive everything we need for life and godliness (2 Peter 1:3), but we may still struggle because our spirit is not in the lead. What we give the most attention to will become the most influential. Our spirit can take the lead only if we feed it more than our soul and body.

The world around us constantly feeds our souls through things we see and hear. And our bodies, if starved, make it known that they're hungry. If we withhold gratification from our souls and our bodies, they get loud. Our spirit, on the other hand, when not fed, gets quiet. We have to be intentional to feed our spirit.

Ask yourself: *What am I doing to feed my spirit?*

....

....

Who is in control?

The soul and the body are complex and can often be confusing, especially since we are accustomed to them taking the lead. Let's consider the following: Very early in life we learn to take instruction from our souls. We have all seen the toddler throw himself on the floor and demand his own way. He is being led by his emotions when he holds his breath until the parent gives in to his demands. We might think that this only happens in the lives of children, but adults can possess the same tendencies.

Read *Galatians 5:19–21 and list the works of the soul-led nature.*

....

....

When the Holy Spirit controls our lives, He will produce this kind of fruit in us: love, joy, peace, patience, kindness, goodness, faithfulness, gentleness, and self-control. (Galatians 5:22–23)

According to Galatians 6:8, what is the result of living a life that gratifies the body? What happens to a person who lives a spirit-led life?

....

....

Daily Living

> Pray that the Lord would eliminate any areas of Pride out.

Living in spiritual order brings with it incredible benefits, such as protection, spiritual growth, and power to overcome obstacles in our lives. And it's important to understand that living out of spiritual order is dangerous. When we allow our soul or body to lead, it opens a door for the enemy to operate in our lives. We will be protected from the enemy when we choose to do things God's way and give control of our lives to Him.

Read Psalm 91. According to verses 9 and 10, who will receive the benefits of protection and safety?

....

....

We want to do things God's way, but what happens when we fall short or give in to temptation? We respond by distancing ourselves from God. We feel shame and condemnation, but that's Tree of the Knowledge of Good and Evil thinking. Remember, God convicts; He does not condemn. Godly sorrow for sin will lead us to repentance, which means "to turn and go the other way."

Write Psalm 66:18-20

....

....

When you realize you're out of spiritual order, stop and repent. Then, ask for and receive His grace. It is the kindness of the Lord that leads us to repentance (Romans 2:4). Remember: He is the God who came looking for Adam and Eve.

Staying in Order

We face decisions every single day, and the choices we make dictate the lives we lead. So how do we make good decisions? We need to change the way we think.

Knowing your identity is also a key to being led by the Holy Spirit. Think about who you are in Him.

Write 2 Corinthians 5:17

....

....

Write Ephesians 1:4

....

....

To walk in spiritual order, we need the power of the Holy Spirit. He is our counselor, our friend, our guide, and the One who reveals truth. Start getting to know Him today. As you grow in your relationship with Him, Bible reading will become more enjoyable, worship more intimate, prayer more powerful, and living in the Tree of Life more tangible and exciting. When you walk with Jesus, life is abundant indeed—and this is only the beginning!

Journal

SECTION TWO

OVERFLOW OF THE HEART

WEEK FIVE
OVERFLOW OF THE HEART

"My son, pay attention to what I say; turn your ear to my words.
Do not let them out of your sight, keep them within your heart; for they are life
to those who find them and health to one's whole body.
Above all else, guard your heart, for everything you do flows from it."

PROVERBS 4:20-23 NIV

"...The Lord does not look at the things people look at.
People look at the outward appearance, but the Lord looks at the heart."

1 SAMUEL 16:7 NIV

FOUR BLOCKAGES OF THE HEART

1. _____

   "But if you harbor bitter envy and selfish ambition in your hearts, do not boast about it or deny the truth. Such "wisdom" does not come down from heaven but is earthly, unspiritual, and demonic. For where you have envy and selfish ambition, there you find disorder and every evil practice.
   JAMES 3:14-16 NIV

2. _____

   "Then He said to the disciples, 'It is impossible that no offenses should come...'"
   LUKE 17:1 NKJV

   "A brother wronged is more unyielding than a fortified city; disputes are like the barred gates of a citadel."
   PROVERBS 18:19 NIV

3. _____

   "The tongue has the power of life and death, and those who love it will eat its fruit."
   PROVERBS 18:21 NIV

4. _____

   "For it is from within, out of a person's heart, that evil thoughts come—sexual immorality, theft, murder, adultery, greed, malice, deceit, lewdness, envy, slander, arrogance and folly. All these evils come from inside and defile a person."
   MARK 7:21-23 NIV

THREE STEPS TO TRANSFORMING THE HEART

> *I will give you a new heart and put a new spirit in you; I will remove from you your heart of stone and give you a heart of flesh. And I will put my Spirit in you and move you to follow my decrees and be careful to keep my laws.*
> EZEKIEL 36:26-27 NIV

1. Invite the Holy Spirit to _____.

   > *"Search me, God, and know my heart; test me and know my anxious thoughts. See if there is any offensive way in me, and lead me in the way everlasting."*
   > PSALM 139:23-24 NIV

2. Invite the Holy Spirit to _____.

   > *"Create in me a pure heart, O God, and renew a steadfast spirit within me. Do not cast me from your presence or take your Holy Spirit from me."*
   > PSALM 51:10-11 NIV

3. Invite the Holy Spirit to _____.

   > *"Do not get drunk on wine, which leads to debauchery. Instead, be filled with the Spirit."*
   > EPHESIANS 5:18 NIV

Journal

WEEK SIX
A LIFE OF SURRENDER

"Trust in the Lord with all your heart and lean not on your own understanding; in all your ways submit to Him, and He will make your paths straight."
PROVERBS 3:5-6 NIV

The word surrender brings to mind many pictures, perhaps a white flag waving atop a surrounded military fort or a troop of outnumbered soldiers with their hands raised. We typically associate surrender with defeat. However, when it comes to life with Christ, the act of giving up control to Him is actually the beginning of our freedom. A life of surrender requires trust, and that trust is developed in the context of relationship. Would you allow a stranger to care for your children or watch over your home while you were on vacation? Of course not. Trust is earned, so until you have an understanding of a person's character, it isn't possible to trust him or her with something of value.

In order to surrender our lives to God, we must believe that He is good and is worthy of our trust. For many of us, that is easier said than done, and it is often due to doubt or disappointment from past experiences with people or churches. Our hearts can become weary and hardened by such things, but there is hope! We can begin to trust Jesus when we understand what He did for us. He left heaven and came to earth; He felt hunger, hurt, and rejection; He was beaten and crucified, and three days later rose from the grave—all so He could prove His love, earn our trust, and be in relationship with us.

Write Psalm 119:68

....

....

If you want to get to know God better, you will need to do what you would do when getting to know a friend: spend time with Him. This doesn't have to look a certain way. The key is to invite Him into your life. The Lord will reveal Himself to you as you do things that feed your spirit, like studying the Word, seeking Him in prayer, and building relationships with like-minded friends.

Write James 4:8

....

....

"For just as the heavens are higher than the earth, so my ways are higher than your ways and my thoughts higher than your thoughts."
ISAIAH 55:9

Sometimes, God's way of doing things doesn't make sense to us. His way of thinking is much different—and much greater—than ours. Though we don't always understand, when we make the choice to trust and obey Him, we set ourselves up for success.

Picture this: You're going to take a road trip to see the Grand Canyon, and you plan to drive your car—but you don't have a smartphone, map, or compass for the trip. Your best friend not only has all of these items, but also knows every pothole, gas station, and restaurant along the way. Wouldn't you want him to come along? What if he has a single condition for joining you: to be in the driver's seat? There's the dilemma. It's hard to hand over the steering wheel because it involves giving up control. However, as a believer, the only way you can live the abundant life that God has for you is to fully surrender your life to Him and adopt His way of doing things.

Ask Yourself: *What areas of my life have I not surrendered to God? Am I having a hard time trusting Him with those areas?*

AN EPIC JOURNEY

God wants to make our lives smoother by being Lord over everything. It is only when He is in control that we can walk in spiritual order. Anything we decide to hold on to becomes our responsibility to maintain. However, if we surrender every area of our lives to Him, He will partner with us on this journey and bring us safely to our final destination.

Write *Luke 14:33*

Man was created to be a worshipper and we will worship what we value most. In Exodus 20:3-4, God told the Israelites not to place any gods before Him or make any kind of idol. We may think of an idol as a carved statue, but an idol is also anything we desire more than God. If we want to walk in spiritual order, God must be first.

Materialism is a common culprit of misplaced priorities in our lives. When material things become most important to us, we find ourselves consumed by pressure and stress as we strive to gain more. Materialism gives the enemy an opening to attack our minds and emotions with incessant thoughts about what we have and what we want. The more we have, the more it demands our attention.

Read the following verses. What happens when we give things and money the place of priority in our lives?

MATTHEW 13:22

REVELATION 3:17

1 TIMOTHY 6:9-10

Ask yourself: Is there anything in my life that is more important than God?

....

....

Read the following verses: Psalm 62:10, Hebrews 13:5 and Luke 12:22-31. Ask the Holy Spirit to show you how these passages apply to your life.

....

....

> *"Seek the Kingdom of God above all else, and live righteously, and He will give you everything you need."*
> **MATTHEW 6:33**

RELATIONSHIP PROBLEMS

Did you know that relationships can come between you and God? It can be relationships with family, friends, co-workers, pastors, church members, neighbors, and even enemies. But whether good or bad, they can become more important to us than our relationship with the Lord.

Read Genesis 22:1–18. In this passage, Abraham faces an inconceivable situation. He has waited decades for a big promise to be fulfilled—the promise that he would be the father of nations. In Abraham's old age, God blesses him with a son, Isaac. The child grows and so does Abraham's joy. And then, one day, God tells Abraham to sacrifice the boy on an altar. Surely Abraham had questions. He loved his son very much—but he also trusted God.

The Bible tells us Abraham rose early the next morning to obey God's command. In other words, he did not try to delay or find a way out. There was no hesitation in his conduct. In a great act of faith, he placed Isaac on the altar and would have followed through with the command if an angel had not stopped him. God saw Abraham's willingness to obey, provided an alternate sacrifice, and blessed him with a family heritage unlike any other. His descendants would be as numerous as the stars in the sky and the sand on the shores.

We often insist on having our own way in relationships, not realizing that our attempts to control them may be detrimental. Not only are our relationships unlikely to flourish when we try to control them, they can take our focus off of God and take inappropriate priority in our lives. As was true for Abraham, God's blessing can flow into our relationships if we readily surrender them to Him.

Ask Yourself: *Do I have a relationship that has come between God and me?*

Another principle that will allow us to have healthy relationships is staying free of offense. Our most difficult relationships to surrender may be the ones in which there is offense and unforgiveness.

Consider this: What if you gave up your "right to be right" and instead chose to be unoffended, no matter the situation?

Six Ways to Stay Unoffended

1. **Take the lowest seat.**
   Consider everyone more important than yourself. Put the needs of others before your own. Strive to please God, not yourself or others. Be a servant, and look to honor others rather than yourself.

2. **Always remain grateful.**
   Gratitude changes our attitude by keeping us aware of God's provision and blessings.

3. **Give others their freedom.**
   Don't try to control others. People need the freedom to make their own decisions. Sometimes they make good ones; sometimes they make bad ones. Either way, it is their decision.

4. **Make decisions that promote life in others.**
   When someone offends you, it may seem natural to ignore that person or pay back wrong, but Jesus says there is a better way. Maintain a positive attitude toward them. Choose to speak words of life over them and do things that build them up. How they respond is up to them.

5. **Trust God to bring justice when an offense comes.**
   Vengeance belongs to the Lord. Think about what it would be like to pay for your own sin, rather than Jesus taking care of it. None of us want what we really deserve. We'd rather have grace!

6. **Dedicate time to the Lord.**
   Refresh your spirit in prayer, Bible study, and fellowship with Jesus. God's presence brings change.

I SURRENDER ALL

There are many areas of our lives that we need to surrender to God. These include plans, goals, pleasures, ambitions, hurts, the future, the past, selfishness, ego, sin, pride, physical appearance, lust, anger, fear, and health. We must also surrender unforgiveness, because holding on to an offense is essentially saying that we have a right to withhold grace from someone. This type of pride is an idol that will cause a wedge between God and us.

Surrendering does not mean we no longer have goals or ambitions. On the contrary, God is the One who puts desires in our hearts. When we surrender everything to Him, we will find that His path to the fulfillment of those desires is better than we could have imagined on our own. We simply have to submit to God's will and join with Him in His plans for us.

Ask Yourself: Have I surrendered my past, present, and future to God? Do I trust that His way is better than my own?

Journal

WEEK SEVEN
FORGIVENESS

"He is so rich in kindness and grace that He purchased our freedom with the blood of his Son and forgave our sins."
EPHESIANS 1:7

Because we live in a fallen world, we face the realities of hurt and offense. The words and deeds of others can wound us to the core in indescribable ways. Things like neglect, abuse, violence, betrayal, and cruel remarks can cause bitterness and resentment to infiltrate our hearts, and we, perhaps even unintentionally, begin to harbor unforgiveness.

An unforgiven offense is like an arrow dipped in poison. The offense slashes through our defenses and hurts us in the moment, but the aftermath of unforgiveness is like a poison that remains long after the event takes place. It seeps into our lives, tainting our thoughts and clouding our vision. If left unchecked, it will eventually penetrate our hearts and paralyze our ability to live, to love, and to be loved. Harboring unforgiveness is like drinking poison and expecting another person to die; it does much greater harm to us than the person we refuse to forgive.

Write Proverbs 18:19

Offense is the bait that the enemy uses to lure us into bondage. When we become offended, we become unyielding. Think about a city surrounded by walls. The walls' purpose is to protect the city. We use this same thinking to protect ourselves, placing walls around our hearts. People may have hurt us once, but we will not allow them to do it again. But what works for a city of stone does not necessarily work in the same way for a heart of flesh and blood. Walls may keep out the bad stuff, but they also keep out the good. With walls around our hearts, we not only protect ourselves from pain and rejection but from experiencing love and life-giving relationships. We think it is up to us to protect our hearts, but the truth is, God never meant for this to be our responsibility; it is His.

Ask Yourself: *Am I harboring unforgiveness?*

Unforgiveness holds us in bondage and keeps us from living in the Tree of Life. So why is it so hard to forgive others? Here are a few possible explanations.

REASONS WE MAY STRUGGLE TO FORGIVE

1. **We have a wrong idea of forgiveness.**

The first reason we don't offer forgiveness easily to others is that we have an incorrect definition of forgiveness. To truly understand what it means to forgive someone, we need to start by learning what forgiveness is not.

- **Forgiveness is not minimizing the offense.**
  Offering forgiveness to someone who has wronged you is not saying, "It's not a big deal," or, "It didn't really hurt." What was done or said was not right, and harm never reflects the Father's heart for you; God's perfect will is to protect you and nurture you. When you choose to forgive, you choose not to hang on to the offense because it robs you of freedom.

- **Forgiveness is not forgetting what happened.**
  Sometimes we think in order to forgive someone, we must forget what has happened. "Forgive and forget" is a cliché that holds no truth. The reality is we may never forget what has happened to us. But, God wants to do something extraordinary in our lives. He wants to bring healing to our hearts so that we can remember these past experiences without reliving the pain associated with them. God wants to show you how he can make all things new.

- **Forgiveness is not reconciliation.**

    We often make reconciliation a caveat for our forgiveness, saying, "When they apologize, I will forgive them." In doing so, we actually become a hostage to the very one who has wronged us because it leaves our freedom up to another person. Letting go of offense does not mean that you must reconcile with the person. Romans 12:18 says, "If it is possible, as far as it depends on you, live at peace with everyone." God understands that there are times when reconciliation may not be the best choice. If the offender is not ready to reconcile, it will only cause further pain and disappointment when you are exposed to the same circumstances. In such situations, rely on the Holy Spirit to lead you. Begin by allowing the miracle of forgiveness to happen in you.

    > Reconciliation is a two-way street. If you've forgiven someone and desire to restore the relationship, use wisdom throughout the process. The door to reconciliation may be open if you see the following in the other person:
    >
    > - *Repentance: Turning away from wrong actions and going in the opposite direction*
    > - *Restitution: Making things right if possible*
    > - *Rebuilding Trust: Proving themselves consistent in words and actions*

2. We don't think it's fair.

The second reason we don't offer forgiveness to those who have hurt us is that it does not seem fair to let them off the hook. We reason in our minds that they don't deserve forgiveness. But God doesn't use "fairness" logic (or doesn't hand out forgiveness based on merit)—and thank goodness, because none of us deserve forgiveness!

Read Matthew 18:21-35. *Through this parable, Jesus explains the profound and undeserved forgiveness we receive as believers. What instruction does Jesus give us regarding forgiveness?*

....

....

Jesus told Peter that he needed to forgive 490 times a day. That's once every three minutes! Considering how fast our minds often race, that number doesn't seem too farfetched, does it? In the Parable of the Unforgiving Debtor, the first man owed the king millions of dollars, but when he begged for mercy, the king canceled his debt. As sinners, we too owed a great debt that we could not pay. But God showed us great mercy and, by the blood of Jesus, paid our debt in full. We have been forgiven much.

The second man owed the first man a debt of a few thousand dollars. While this is not an insignificant amount of money, the first man was forgiven a much greater debt. In light of the incredible mercy he was shown by the king, he should have readily shown mercy to the second man as well. Since we have been forgiven so very much, we should extend what we have received to others. The forgiven must forgive!

> **Ask Yourself:** *In light of all the sin for which I have been forgiven, can I release those who have wronged me? Would I trade my forgiveness from God for the right to hold someone accountable for their offense toward me?*

3. We don't think we can do it.

The third reason we don't forgive is that we don't think we have the power and strength to do so. This is the voice of the enemy. We must recognize and silence the voice of our adversary. In our own human power, we may not be strong enough to forgive the great wrongs done against us, but we don't have to walk through this Christian life in our own strength.
We are empowered by the supernatural strength of God.

Write 2 Corinthians 12:9

In this passage, Paul is saying something incredible happens in the midst of his struggles—the power of Christ is at work! Forgiveness does not turn us into doormats. On the contrary, forgiveness makes us victorious.

Forgiveness is a choice, not a feeling, and it is a choice we have to make daily. We prefer to wait until we feel like forgiving, but if our lives are dictated by our feelings, we will always live according to the reality of this world. God is inviting you into a new reality.

If we dare to believe God, and choose first to forgive, our feelings will follow our decision. Then, instead of merely "reacting" to what happens to us, we can choose to live in the Tree of Life. Remember: Choices lead, feelings follow.

THE FORGIVEN FORGIVE

We forgive others in response to the great forgiveness we've been shown by Jesus. Read Isaiah 1:18–19. This passage says that our sins were scarlet, and Jesus made them white as snow; they were crimson, and He made them as wool. Note that the end of the Scripture says "if you obey me." Forgiveness is not a suggestion, but a requirement from our loving Father for our benefit. The forgiven forgive.

> *"Get rid of all bitterness, rage, anger, harsh words, and slander, as well as all types of evil behavior. Instead, be kind to each other, tenderhearted, forgiving one another, just as God through Christ has forgiven you."*
> **EPHESIANS 4:31-32**

Romans 5:6 says that while we were still sinners, God sent Jesus to die for us. When it comes to understanding forgiveness, this is critical: It is impossible to forgive others of their offenses until we receive forgiveness for ourselves. If we struggle with forgiveness, chances are we have not fully grasped what God has done for us. We have been given total forgiveness for past, present and future sin. It is not that God forgets our sins, but, rather, He chooses to remember our sin no more. He chooses to never mention our sin again—ever. Why does He do this? Because God desperately wants to be in relationship with us.

Write Isaiah 43:25

....

....

The Unforgiveness Trap

An offense is something we consider to be a violation of what we think is right and fair. We need to understand that the enemy uses offense to hold us captive and keep us from moving forward in the freedom that God has for us. The word offense comes from the Greek word *"scandalon,"* which means "the bait." In Old Testament times, when someone wanted to trap an animal, they would cover a pit with branches and place a piece of flesh (scandalon) on top of the branches to lure the animal into the trap.

Satan uses offense as bait to lure us into a trap of unforgiveness and bondage. By holding on to offense, we think we are trapping the person who hurt us, but in reality, we are the ones who are ensnared.

Below is a list of five common snares that the enemy uses to lure us into unforgiveness. Notice that Jesus Himself also suffered these offenses. Jesus was fully God and fully man. He allowed Himself to be tempted in every way that we are today because He wanted us to know that no matter what we face, He has been there—and He has overcome.

When we are…
Betrayed – by a best friend who lied, a spouse who didn't stay forever, a confidant who broke our trust
Falsely Accused – misunderstood, the subject of gossip and slander
Rejected – by a spouse, friend, trusted authority, or even a church
Abused – emotionally, physically, verbally, or sexually
Humiliated – haunted by an embarrassing moment, ashamed, disgraced

Remember Jesus was…
Betrayed – by Judas, a trusted friend and one of His disciples
Falsely Accused – wrongly indicted in several courts
Rejected – by Peter, one of His disciples and closest companions
Abused – beaten, tortured, cursed, and crucified on a cross
Humiliated – crucified and disgraced in a public setting

To get a better understanding of why Jesus had to suffer in the way He did, read Hebrews 2:17–18 in The Message translation:

"That's why He had to enter into every detail of human life. Then, when He came before God as high priest to get rid of the people's sins, He would have already experienced it all Himself—all the pain, all the testing—and would be able to help where help was needed."

It was important for Jesus to experience all of these offenses in a human body so that He could understand every struggle we would encounter. Now, when we come to Him with our hurts, He can honestly reply, "I understand. I went through that, too." Not only is Jesus now able to empathize with our pain, but because He went through these trials, He was able to set an example for how we should respond when we suffer at the hands of others.

At His death, Jesus asked the Father to forgive the very ones who cursed Him, who nailed His hands and feet to the cross, saying, "They don't know what they are doing." (Luke 23:34) In reality, they knew exactly what they were doing: killing a man they hated and making sure He felt every ounce of their malice. Jesus knew his oppressors were blinded by hate, but He chose to view their actions with a heavenly perspective. Offenses will undoubtedly come, so we must arm ourselves with the same thinking of Jesus.

Our primary prayer in relationships should be that the Lord would allow us to see the other person through the eyes of Jesus. If we begin to see others as God sees them, we will find ourselves loving people the way Jesus did, regardless of what they do or don't do to us.

Living an Unoffended Life

How do we keep our hearts pure and unoffended? Consider these three simple statements:

1. Recognize our own imperfection.

We will never have to forgive others for more than God has forgiven us.

Write Romans 3:23

....

....

Write Matthew 10:8

....

....

2. Focus on the real enemy.

People are not our enemy—the devil is. Jesus made a choice to see the people with the hammer and nails as unknowing participants in satan's agenda of darkness. If it is true that hurting people hurt people, then the guilty have their own story as well. Our approach should be to love people and hate the devil.

Write 1 Peter 5:8

....

....

3. Receive the love of God.

This will give us the capacity to love people. If we continually struggle to love people, it may be because we have not fully received the love of God.

Write 1 John 4:10

....

....

FORGIVENESS IN ACTION

The Bible's steps for walking out forgiveness are countercultural (the opposite of mainstream society) and counterintuitive (different than what would be expected). But if you follow them, they will change your life. Our way of thinking and God's way of thinking are not the same. Read 1 Corinthians 1:25–28 (NIV) to gain the proper perspective on submitting to God's way of doing things:

"For the foolishness of God is wiser than human wisdom, and the weakness of God is stronger than human strength. Brothers and sisters, think of what you were when you were called. Not many of you were wise by human standards; not many were influential; not many were of noble birth. But God chose the foolish things of the world to shame the wise; God chose the weak things of the world to shame the strong. God chose the lowly things of this world and the despised things—and the things that are not—to nullify the things that are."

Daily Steps for Walking Out Forgiveness

1. Pray for people who have offended you.

Society tells us to return evil for evil or, at the very least, isolate the people who hurt us so they cannot do so again. But Jesus said in order to have different results, we have to respond differently.

Write Matthew 5:43-44

2. Bless people who have offended you.

For some of us, it is all we can do not to talk negatively about the people who have wronged us. But Jesus asks us to go a step further; He asks us to bless them. The word bless means to "speak well of." Again, this is not something that is demonstrated in today's culture. Listen to what the Bible says:

> *"But to you who are willing to listen, I say, love your enemies! Do good to those who hate you. Bless those who curse you. Pray for those who hurt you."*
> LUKE 6:27-28

Write Romans 12:14

....

....

3. Do good to people who have offended you.

This requires a change in our way of thinking. It is not that we are repaying good for evil; it is that we have made the decision to do only good to others. So whether someone is serving or attacking us, our response should be to treat them well, as the Word says to do.

Ask yourself: Are there people in my life who I have not released to the Lord? Am I trying to get revenge for their offense?

....

....

LET FREEDOM RING

Below is a declaration based on Romans 12:17–21. Read it out loud.

I do not repay evil for evil. I am careful to do what is right in the eyes of everyone. If it is possible, as far as it depends on me, I will live at peace with everyone. I will not take revenge, but leave room for God's wrath, because God has promised He will handle it. On the contrary: If my enemy is hungry, I will feed him; if he is thirsty, I will give him something to drink. I will not be overcome by evil, but I will overcome evil with good.

A PRAYER OF FORGIVENESS

This is a simple prayer of forgiveness you can use to release anyone who has offended you. Insert the name or names of those you feel you need to forgive, and say the words out loud.

"Lord, instead of loving, I have resented certain people, and I have unforgiveness in my heart. Forgive me for my sin of holding on to offense. I ask you, Lord, to give me the power to forgive those who have hurt me. I release them to you now. Give me the strength to pray for them, bless them, and want the best for them. Thank you for breaking these chains off of my life. In the name of Jesus I pray, Amen."

FORGIVING OURSELVES

Getting past your past may be the biggest obstacle you face. Every time you seem to be making progress, that old movie reel of the sinful things you have done begins to play in your mind. Peace and freedom slip away as your past rises up to remind you of your failure. You think forgiveness is for other people but not for you because you have done too many horrible things and it's just too late.

You may be surprised to know that these feelings are actually common for many believers. The enemy loves to remind us of the mistakes we made in the past because guilt keeps us stuck, unable to move forward into the future that God has planned for us. We feel we must repent for our past over and over again as we are continually bombarded by painful memories that we are powerless to change. These thoughts come solely from the Tree of the Knowledge of Good and Evil.

Ask Yourself: Am I constantly reminding myself of past failures? Does the sin of my past continue to bother me even though I have asked God to forgive me?

Confronting The Past

When our past rears its ugly head, there are three ways we usually respond:

1. **We try to bury it.**
    Have you ever heard the phrase, "You've got to bury the past"? Well, the fact is, you can't. It will find its way to the surface at some point. We hear that time heals all wounds, but that is also untrue. Only the Holy Spirit can heal. Concealing the past never works. Proverbs 28:13 (NIV) says, "Whoever conceals their sins does not prosper, but the one who confesses and renounces them finds mercy." The Bible also says that confessing our sins and praying for one another actually helps us find healing and wholeness. (James 5)

2. **We beat ourselves up.**
    Some of us live in the land of regret. We dwell on the "if only" scenarios from our past. But "if only" is a trap. We cannot change the past and the enemy uses the notion to torment us. King David knew this type of grief. He committed adultery with his own soldier's wife and then had the soldier killed when she became pregnant with his child. When the prophet Nathan confronted David, he repented and cried out to God. In Psalm 38:4–8, David says, "My guilt overwhelms me—it is a burden too heavy to bear. My wounds fester and stink because of my foolish sins. I am bent over and racked with pain. All day long I walk around filled with grief. A raging fever burns within me, and my health is broken. I am exhausted and completely crushed. My groans come from an anguished heart." David shows us that unwillingness to forgive ourselves can even cause physical pain in addition to emotional pain.

3. **We blame others.**

    This tactic has been used since the days of Adam and Eve. When God asked Adam why he disobeyed, Adam blamed Eve. Eve's response was to blame the serpent. (Genesis 3:12–13) We must take responsibility for our actions, then repent and move forward.

Since these are unhealthy ways to deal with our past, what is the best way to face it? We need to look to the Word and agree with God's perspective on our past. God says when we ask Jesus into our hearts, our old life vanishes and we become a new person. You may know this in your head, but is it your reality?

> *"Anyone who belongs to Christ has become a new person. The old life is gone; a new life has begun!"*
> 2 CORINTHIANS 5:17

The Apostle Paul had a terrible past of persecuting and killing Christians, but he understood this truth, and it allowed him to accept the grace of God and move forward in freedom.

> *"Even though I was once a blasphemer and a persecutor and a violent man, I was shown mercy because I acted in ignorance and unbelief. The grace of our Lord was poured out on me abundantly, along with the faith and love that are in Christ Jesus. Here is a trustworthy saying that deserves full acceptance: Christ Jesus came into the world to save sinners—of whom I am the worst."*
> 1 TIMOTHY 1:13-15 NIV

Getting Past the Past

To let our past die, we must change our way of thinking. The old way of thinking doesn't line up with God's Word, so it doesn't produce life. We must accept what the Bible says and renew our minds with the truth so that we, like Paul, can walk in freedom. In order to walk in freedom from our past, we need to do the following:

1. **Stop trying to earn forgiveness.**
   Most people don't understand the gospel. They think that if they work hard to be good more days than they are bad, they get to go to heaven. That's not true. The price has been paid. Forgiveness is received, not earned. If we think we have to earn forgiveness from God, we will make others earn forgiveness from us.

   Here is the gospel:

   "For it is by grace you have been saved, through faith—and this is not from yourselves, it is the gift of God—not by works, so that no one can boast."
   EPHESIANS 2:8-9 NIV

2. **Receive God's forgiveness by faith.**
   It will free our hearts and allow us to forgive others.

3. **Defeat every lie with the truth.**

   It would be great if once we had received forgiveness, we never thought about our past again. The truth is, the enemy will continue to bring up our past every day. He will wait for weak moments in our lives and whisper our failures to us. We have to resist him every day. Remember, he is the accuser of Christians and the "Father of Lies." (Revelation 12:10) We defeat him by knowing and speaking the truth.

Write 1 Corinthians 1:30

....

Write Romans 8:28

....

God never said that forgiveness would be easy. In fact, following the instructions in His Word takes courage and strength. But His instructions work. They will lead us into pathways of righteousness where we can live again, free from the ghosts of our past. No more guilt, no more hiding, no more shame. Free.

It takes faith to believe that these words are true, but if you do, they will change your life. Trust that God's Word is true. Believe that you have been made new and clean and that He can and will make you whole again. Life as you know it will never be the same. As you begin to see yourself the way God sees you, you will begin to see others differently. You'll find yourself with open hands, releasing offenses, and receiving abundant life. You will be living in the Tree of Life.

Journal

WEEK EIGHT
THE POWER OF WORDS

"Death and life are in the power of the tongue."
PROVERBS 18:21 NKJV

The words we speak are a spiritual gauge, showing how much of our soul we have surrendered to God. If we have allowed our minds to be renewed by the Word, our conversation can't help but reflect what we have learned. If, on the other hand, we are hesitant to release our old habits and beliefs, our words will betray us and reveal our true spiritual condition. If our souls are not in submission to God and we haven't surrendered everything to Him, our tongues will be the first to sell us out.

Write *Luke 6:45*

Read *Matthew 12:34-35. What does Jesus say about the relationship between our hearts and what we say?*

Ask Yourself: *What does my day-to-day conversation say about my spiritual condition? Do my words reflect that God lives inside of me?*

Jesus tells us that a life consumed with the cares and treasures of the world will lead to fruitless talk that will bring judgment upon us. A life surrendered to God and filled with the Holy Spirit will produce speech full of grace, mercy, love, and power.

THE POWER OF GOD'S WORDS

> *"By faith we understand that the entire universe was formed at God's command, that what we now see did not come from anything that can be seen."*
> **HEBREWS 11:3**

With words, God spoke the entire universe into being. With words, He communicates to us. Through the Bible, with its thousands of words, He reveals Himself to us. John 1:1 says that Jesus is actually the living, breathing Word of God. Words and language were His idea, and His words are literally life to us. Because God created man in His image, our words have power. Since Jesus is our example in everything, and we are to follow in His steps, let's look at a few verses that demonstrate the power of His words. In the following verses, underline what happened when Jesus spoke.

Matthew 8:26 – *Jesus responded, "Why are you afraid? You have so little faith!" Then He got up and rebuked the wind and waves, and suddenly there was a great calm."*

Matthew 8:32 – *"'All right, go!' Jesus commanded them. So the demons came out of the men..."*

John 11:43–44 (ESV) – *When he said these things, he cried out with a loud voice, "Lazarus, come out." The man who had died came out."*

As you can see in these verses, the spoken Word of God can bring healing, peace, deliverance, and life!

TWO KINGDOMS

Isaiah 14 recounts the fall of satan. Verses 12–14 say, "How you are fallen from heaven, O shining star, son of the morning! You have been thrown down to the earth, you who destroyed the nations of the world. For you said to yourself, 'I will ascend to heaven and set my throne above God's stars. I will preside on the mountain of the gods far away in the north. I will climb to the highest heavens and be like the Most High.'" (NKJV) Through the power of satan's spoken words of rebellion, the kingdom of darkness was established. And he actually spoke the first words of rebellion in his heart. Satan and his demons continue to speak words of rebellion to our minds. If we aren't enlightened to this truth, we will be his advocate in hurting others and even ourselves with the words that we speak. Every time we open our mouths to talk, we either advance the kingdom of life or we advance the kingdom of death.

When we were saved, we weren't taken directly to heaven because we are Jesus' body—His hands, feet, heart, and mouth designed to reach the lost and make a difference in this world. But we can't advance the Kingdom of Heaven on our own.

Knowing we would need help in order to represent Jesus to the world, God set us up for tremendous success by sending us the Holy Spirit. Jesus told His disciples it would actually be to their advantage if He left and went back to heaven. (John 16:7) Though Jesus was fully God, He was also fully human—He could only be in one place at a time while He walked around in a human body. We can be filled with the Holy Spirit and have Him as our personal guide through life no matter where we are on the earth. Jesus said, "But when He, the Spirit of truth, comes, He will guide you into all the truth; for He will not speak on

His own initiative, but whatever He hears, He will speak; and He will disclose to you what is to come." (John 16:13 NASB) In other words, through the Holy Spirit, God will disclose to us all the guidance we will need, including what to say.

Ask Yourself: Am I intentional to use my words to promote the Kingdom of God and to minister to others?

Control Issues

In the Garden of Eden, satan spoke to Eve to entice her. Eve didn't know it, but when she and Adam had a conversation about satan's idea, she advanced the kingdom of death through her spoken words. God said, "Because you have listened to the voice of your wife, and have eaten from the tree about which I commanded you, saying, 'You shall not eat from it'; cursed is the ground because of you; in toil you will eat of it all the days of your life." (Genesis 3:17 NASB) Satan didn't bring death to Eve by biting her and releasing poisonous venom or by wrapping his coils around her and squeezing the life out of her. He talked her to death. She then proceeded to talk Adam to death by discussing the evil idea. Can you see how important it is to control our words?

Controlling what we say requires us to tame the part of ourselves that contains the power of life and death: our tongues.

> *"We all make many mistakes. For if we could control our tongues, we would be perfect and could also control ourselves in every other way."*
> JAMES 3:2

Some of our greatest hurts and heartaches come from what people have said to us. Conversely, some of our greatest memories center on positive things that people have said to us, like the phrase, "I love you." Those are wonderful words to hear, but for some of us, they are hard to say, even to those we love. Our words can either tear others down or build them up.

Think of all the conversations you have in a given day. Are the words that come out of your mouth reflective of what you say you believe in your heart? As Christians, our words and actions should reflect our love for God. If they don't, it's important to look inward and see where our hearts and our words are not matching up. Jesus' brother James makes the argument that if you say you are a Christian and that you love God, but your attitude and actions reflect something different, you may fall into the category of the deceived. In James 3:2, he says that we can control ourselves in every way if we can control our tongues.

Read the statements below and consider the effect these words of life or words of death can have on someone's life.

Words of life	Words of death
I love you.	I hate you.
You're such a blessing!	I wish you had never been born.
You look great.	You're ugly.
I see potential in you.	You'll never amount to anything.
You're smart.	You're stupid.
You're so thoughtful.	You're selfish.
You can do it!	You shouldn't even try.
You did your best.	You're a failure.
I forgive you.	I never want to see you again.
I'm committed to you.	I want a divorce.
Life is better because of you.	You were a mistake.

TONGUE-TIED

The book of James goes on to talk about the power of the tongue, our spoken words. In chapter three, James tells us that the tongue can defile the whole body, and he uses three vivid images to help us see his point:

1. **A Bit:** The tongue is petite, weighing only about two ounces, but it is powerful. Like the small piece of metal used to steer horses, the tongue can control the direction of our lives. (James 3:3)

2. **A Rudder:** Although ships are typically large and driven by strong winds, they are steered by this very small blade. Too often we focus on the big things and forget that this one little issue of the tongue could determine the direction of our lives. The tongue can control us, or we can use it to control our destiny. (James 3:4)

3. **A Spark:** A spark, though caused by a quick strike, can set off a wild fire. In the same way, what we say might be curt but can be consuming. Some of the most hurtful things that we have said or that have been said to us are sharp one-liners or even one word. These abrupt, rude statements may be quickly forgotten by the one who said them, but the impact stays with the person who receives them. (James 3:5)

Thousands of acres of forest can be destroyed by a fire that hundreds of firefighters cannot extinguish. Similarly, the tongue can cause destruction beyond belief. While at times words can be petty and seemingly insignificant, they can be poisonous. Careless words often cause great harm. Imagine a child struggling to read and a frustrated and worried parent listening to the child twist the words day after day. Finally, after losing all patience, the parent screams, "What's wrong with you? You can't read!" Those words have the potential to make the child feel stupid and give up even trying. Thoughtless words can have a lasting effect that could change the course of a person's life and cause widespread destruction.

Write James 3:7-8

"Sometimes it praises our Lord and Father, and sometimes it curses those who have been made in the image of God. And so blessing and cursing come pouring out of the same mouth. Surely, my brothers and sisters, this is not right! Does a spring of water bubble out with both fresh water and bitter water? Does a fig tree produce olives, or a grapevine produce figs? No, and you can't draw fresh water from a salty spring."
JAMES 3:9-12

Ask yourself: Do I say things about myself, or others, that I quickly regret?

HOW TO TAME THE TONGUE

We need God's help to change the way we speak, but know this: Change is possible. Because we were made in God's image, we were meant to speak words of life that build up, bring healing, and offer encouragement. Let's take a look at a few principles that will help us use words that advance the kingdom of life.

1. **Guard your heart.**

Jesus says in Matthew 12:34, "Whatever is in your heart determines what you say." The words of our mouth reflect our inner condition. If we desire to control our tongue, we need to control the junk that bombards our ears and saturates our souls. Remember, "A good person produces good things from the treasury of a good heart, and an evil person produces evil things from the treasury of an evil heart." (Matthew 12:35) It's the old "garbage in, garbage out" principle.

Write Psalm 51:10

....

....

Some of us grew up in homes where everyone was critical, where belittling remarks were part of the daily routine and yelling was the main form of communication. If you were raised in that kind of environment, you may have already made a decision to do things differently. But maybe you still experience great discouragement after you lash out at someone, wishing you had not acted that way. Because you saw verbal attacks modeled when you were young, you react the same way. This is a vicious cycle that may lead to something called generational sin. Generational sin is passed down from person to person in a family until it is recognized and broken. One of the ways to break the cycle is to put a filter on our minds and protect ourselves from the venomous effects of careless and evil speech.

2. Gauge your tongue.

A gauge is a tool used to measure or determine the maximum amount of something. If we had a gauge on our tongues, we would know when to stop speaking. Colossians 3:8 (NIV) says, "But now you must also rid yourselves of all such things as these: anger, rage, malice, slander, and filthy language from your lips." We must decide that we aren't going to say the things we used to say. We need to make the decision today, and then manage our decision daily.

Write Psalm 141:3

Read Proverbs 10:19. What happens when we talk too much? What do sensible people do?

....

....

3. Garnish your speech.

A garnish is an extra flourish set on a plate to add a pleasing aesthetic to the dish. What would it be like if we decided that before we let anything out of our mouths, we would garnish it to make it sound pleasing to others?

Write Ephesians 4:29

....

....

At times, we need to say things that are difficult or may appear negative, but even so, we can speak in a way that can bless and encourage the other person. Even bad news can be delivered in a life-giving way. Discipline can be given in a way that truly benefits the one being corrected.

Sometimes, the best thing to say is nothing at all. There were plenty of times that Jesus held His tongue, even when He endured absolute brutality. In fact, although He never committed a sin, the Bible says that Jesus learned obedience by the things He suffered. "When being reviled and insulted, He did not revile or insult in return." 1 Peter 2:23 AMP

WISE WORDS

The Proverbs are full of teaching regarding how we should use our tongues.

Read the following Scriptures and write the instruction given.

PROVERBS 4:24

PROVERBS 15:1

PROVERBS 16:13

PROVERBS 16:28

BREAKING THE CURSE

Sometimes, entire families are characterized by certain words. "They're just a bunch of losers. None of them even finished school." "They've always been that way—they say even her grandmother had a bad temper." Sin can be passed from generation to generation, and so can the consequences. (Exodus 20:5) If your family has generational sin in any form, the good news is that you can be freed from it! You can be the first generation to walk in freedom and begin a flow of God's loving kindness and blessing to a thousand generations after you. (Exodus 20:6) Ask God to shine light on words that should never have been spoken to you.

Write down any words of death and cursing that have been spoken to you by others.

....

....

Write down any words of death and cursing that you have spoken to yourself.

Write down any words of death and cursing that you have spoken to others.

The Voice of Victory

If you have been on the receiving end of destructive words, there is good news: You can truly be healed and set free from the effects of those words. Below are four steps you can take to be set free from harmful words that have been spoken over you. Pray through these steps as you begin to identify any lies you have believed.

1. **Confess:** Healing starts with admitting we were wrong. We must first acknowledge that we have believed something that is not true and have agreed with the lies of the enemy.

    "If we confess our sins, He is faithful and just and will forgive us our sins and purify us from all unrighteousness."
    1 JOHN 1:9 NIV

2. **Repent:** To repent means to change direction. When we repent, we choose to turn around and go the opposite way of our previous path. Stop your agreement with the enemy in its tracks and set your mind on a new course of thinking. If anyone has hurt you by reinforcing these lies in your life, forgive them and release them to the Lord.

    "Repent, then, and turn to God, so that your sins may be wiped out, that times of refreshing may come from the Lord."
    ACTS 3:19 NIV

It is important to note that when we confess our sins and reject the enemy's lies, we realign ourselves with God's truth. Armed with confidence in His Word, we can take authority over the enemy and remove the effects of his lies from our lives.

3. **Cast off:** We must refuse to allow the enemy to continue to use destructive words or events against us. With the authority of the Name of Jesus, command the enemy to leave.

    "Submit yourselves, then, to God. Resist the devil, and he will flee from you."
    JAMES 4:7 NIV

4. **Bless:** Once the enemy has been removed, fill the place that he held with truth and promises found in Scripture. Speak life over yourself by declaring an accurate view of how God sees you.

    "For we are God's handiwork, created in Christ Jesus to do good works, which God prepared in advance for us to do."
    EPHESIANS 2:10 NIV

LIFE DECLARATIONS

Read these words aloud, and receive the truth from God's Word:

- I am blessed with God's supernatural wisdom, and I have clear direction for my life.
- I am blessed with creativity, courage, ability, and abundance.
- I am blessed with a strong will, self control, and self discipline.
- I am blessed with great family, good friends, and good health.
- I am blessed with faith, favor, and fulfillment.
- I am blessed with success, supernatural strength, promotion, and divine protection.
- I am blessed with an obedient heart and with a positive outlook on life.
- I declare that any curse that has ever been spoken over me, any negative evil word that has ever come against me, is broken right now in Jesus' name.
- I am blessed wherever I go.
- Everything I put my hands to is going to prosper and succeed.
- I am blessed!

Journal

WEEK NINE
THE LIVING WORD

> *"Be strong and courageous, for you are the one who will lead these people to possess all the land I swore to their ancestors I would give them. Be strong and very courageous. Be careful to obey all the instructions Moses gave you. Do not deviate from them, turning either to the right or to the left. Then you will be successful in everything you do. Study this Book of Instruction continually. Meditate on it day and night so you will be sure to obey everything written in it. Only then will you prosper and succeed in all you do."*
>
> **JOSHUA 1:6-8**

Imagine if someone offered you a special gift that would guarantee you direction, prosperity, and success. A gift that would give you the ability to rise above any circumstance and stand against any enemy. A gift that would keep you from sin, destruction, and despair. Wouldn't you be eager to receive this gift? Well, you can! Through the gift of the Bible, we have access to all of that power. If we read God's Word and apply it to our lives, we will see Him fulfill the promises contained in its pages.

Ask Yourself: *Am I regularly consuming the Word of God and letting its truth replace my old way of thinking?*

Write *John 1:1-3*

Jesus was present at the world's beginning, and He is the Word. Jesus and the Word of God are one and the same, which has profound implications! In Jesus, the Word was manifested in human form, and through the Word, we have Jesus manifested on written pages. If Jesus appeared to you in the flesh right now and someone around you was sick or depressed, you probably wouldn't have any trouble believing that Jesus could heal them and set them free. The same power that is in Jesus is in the Word. The Word of God is powerful! We have to receive that truth in order for the Word to work in our lives. If at some point we feel the Word has lost its power, it's not because the Word has changed, it's because we've stopped mixing the Word with faith. If you want to fall in love with Jesus, find Him in the Word, and make the Word a priority in your life. If you want more power, consume more of His Word. Then the Word will come alive.

Write John 6:63

....

....

The word Spirit is *"pneuma"* in the Greek, and it means "the Presence or breath of God." The Bible is not just a collection of words in a book that you can study to improve your life; instead, it is a powerful body of truth—the very breath of God—that has the ability to bring about its own fulfillment.

Write Isaiah 55:11

....

....

The Word is literally Spirit and life. If you try to understand the Bible with only your mind, it will be dry and without power. Studying the Word is important, but if we don't include the Spirit of God in the process, the words we read will be exactly that—just words on a page. If your experience with the Bible has been unexciting up to this point, rest assured you are not alone. Like trying to read a novel without the correct prescription glasses, many of us are trying to read the Bible without the one thing that will help us see. We need the Spirit of God for the Word to come alive!

> *"But I have a greater witness than John—my teachings and my miracles. The Father gave me these works to accomplish. And they prove that he sent me. And the Father who sent me has testified about me Himself. You have never heard His voice or seen Him face to face, and you do not have his message in your hearts, because you do not believe me—the one he sent to you. You search the Scriptures because you think they give you eternal life. But the Scriptures point to me!"*
>
> **JOHN 5:36-39**

In the New Testament, we often see Pharisees questioning the legitimacy of Jesus' claiming to be the Son of God. The Pharisees were religious scholars who knew the Scriptures better than anyone at that time. They could even recite the first five books of the Old Testament from memory! But in the Scripture above, Jesus points out that there is more to knowing God than intellectually knowing the Scriptures. He confronts the Pharisees, saying "You search the Scriptures because you think they give you eternal life. But the Scriptures point to me!" You are missing the big picture if you're only reading the Word to get a thought for the day.

The Bible can come alive, introduce you to the true character of Jesus, and genuinely change your life.

Ask Yourself: *Am I reading the Bible out of duty or out of desire to know God?*

THE WORD REVEALED

One of the most incredible stories of the Bible is the account of young Mary and her visit with the angel Gabriel who tells her she is about to become the mother of the Savior of the world. Take a look at the details in Luke 1:26–37.

Mary's initial response to the angel was to question how she could bear a child as a virgin. In verse 37, Gabriel says, "Nothing is impossible with God." The word "nothing" in Greek is two words: "*no* ***rhema***." "Rhema" is the Greek word for "word," and it means "revealed word." You may have experienced the rhema Word of God while listening to a sermon: It seemed like the words leapt from the speaker's mouth and landed right in your heart. You may have also experienced rhema while reading your Bible: The words jumped off the page and spoke directly to the battle you were facing. That's the Word at work! When it becomes revelation to you, no word God speaks will be void of the power for its fulfillment.

Write Luke 1:38 and note Mary's response to the angel's news.

After the Word became revelation to Mary, she believed. She had settled in her heart ahead of time that anything God would speak to her would be true. So when the rhema Word came from Gabriel, she was prepared to obey. Have you settled in your heart that once you hear God speak, you will obey? If aspects of the Word don't make sense to you or you're not yet seeing the fulfillment of a Biblical promise, remember that God is not looking for you to understand; He's looking for you to obey. We need to say, "God, I may not understand it, but I choose to trust You anyway."

Can you remember a time when you experienced the rhema Word of God?

....

....

WAYS TO ACTIVATE THE WORD OF GOD IN YOUR LIFE

1. **Make God's Word a priority.**

We will always make time for the things that are important to us. Just as our bodies need food for fuel, our spirits need the Word. As you spend time reading your Bible each day, it will bring you life.

2. **Believe what you read.**

Choose to believe that the Word is true. God says that it is impossible to please Him without faith. If you put your trust in God's Word, you will see your faith and confidence grow as you read it!

> *Faith comes from hearing the message, and the message is heard through the Word about Christ.*
> **ROMANS 10:17 NIV**

3. **Meditate on Scripture.**

Don't just do a daily reading and put the Word away. Think about it. Psalm 1:2 says the righteous man delights in the law of the Lord and meditates on it day and night. The word "meditate" means "chew the cud." In other words, you should get the nutrients out of it and swallow it—then, recall it again and chew on it some more. Chew on it all day long, and you'll be mindful of it and able to do what it says. Consistently recalling truth to mind paves the way for rhema or revelation to take place and puts faith into motion.

WAYS TO MEDITATE ON THE WORD OF GOD

1. **Speak God's Word out loud.**

Find declarations in Scripture that you can speak out loud to strengthen your spirit. Saying Scripture out loud effectively reminds your soul of what is true, and when the Word comes out of your mouth, it will build your faith. Memorize truth and promises from the Word so that you can speak specific Scripture over specific situations. For example, when you are battling the enemy, use a verse like 1 John 4:4 (NASB), "Greater is He who is in me than he who is in the world." If the passage is not in first person, make it personal. Read Luke 10:19 like this: God has given me "authority to trample on snakes and scorpions and to overcome all the power of the enemy; nothing will harm me." When your circumstances appear overwhelming, remind yourself, out loud, of the truth. In the appendix, you will find Scripture to help you in situations you may face.

Write the following verses in first person, making them personal to you. Then say them out loud.

ROMANS 8:37

PSALM 27:1

PSALM 103:3

PHILIPPIANS 4:19

2. Think about the Word day and night.

If you are tuned in to God for only one of your sixteen waking hours, the world may often seem more real to you than God and His truth because you are spending much more time in the world. Bring your world and God's world together and make them one. Your secular world shouldn't be any different than your sacred world.

3. Make meditation practical.

When it comes to meditation, frequency is key. It's not how much, it's how often. Reading through the Bible three times a year may be a great goal, but it will be meaningless if you aren't taking time to allow specific truth to sink into your heart. Learn how to find nuggets and chew on them throughout the day. Choose a verse, and study it. Recite it to yourself. Talk about it with your friends. Write it down in a journal. Post it on your refrigerator or bathroom mirror. It may be more beneficial to read a specific verse ten times a day rather than reading for 30 minutes.

In Proverbs 3:1–4, underline what we need to do with God's words.

My child, never forget the things I have taught you. Store my commands in your heart. If you do this, you will live many years, and your life will be satisfying. Never let loyalty and kindness leave you! Tie them around your neck as a reminder. Write them deep within your heart. Then you will find favor with both God and people, and you will earn a good reputation.

Read Psalm 119:97-100 and list the benefits of meditating on God's Word.

DO WHAT IS WRITTEN

There may be times when we are actively studying the Word, learning its truth, and getting excited about it, but do we consistently do what it says? What would it be like if we began putting what the Bible says into practice every day? We would see the truth of the Word at work in our lives. The promises of God are fulfilled when we walk in obedience to His Word.

Read James 1:22. According to this verse, how can we deceive ourselves?

In James 1:23–25 (NLT), we find a premise to the promise of seeing God's power work in our lives. "For if you listen to the Word and don't obey, it is like glancing at your face in a mirror. You see yourself, walk away, and forget what you look like. But if you look carefully into the perfect law that sets you free, and if you do what it says and don't forget what you heard, then God will bless you for doing it."

Make your daily time in the Word sacred. Don't let anything interrupt. Find one verse that resonates with you, say it out loud, think about it all day long, put it into practice, and see what happens.

Meditation will turn into revelation.

Revelation will activate your faith.

When your faith is activated, things change!

Journal

SECTION THREE

VESSELS OF HONOR

WEEK TEN
VESSELS OF HONOR

God anointed Jesus of Nazareth with the Holy Spirit and power, and how He went around doing good and healing all who were under the power of the devil, because God was with Him.

ACTS 10:38 NIV

THREE THINGS TO KNOW

1. Demons are _____.

   Then war broke out in heaven. Michael and his angels fought against the dragon, and the dragon and his angels fought back. But he was not strong enough, and they lost their place in heaven. The great dragon was hurled down—that ancient serpent called the devil, or Satan, who leads the whole world astray. He was hurled to the earth, and his angels with him.
   REVELATION 12:7-9 NIV

2. Demons want to _____.

   > *Be alert and of sober mind. Your enemy the devil prowls around like a roaring lion looking for someone to devour. Resist him, standing firm in the faith...*
   > **1 PETER 5:8-9 NIV**

   > *Have nothing to do with the fruitless deeds of darkness, but rather expose them.*
   > **EPHESIANS 5:11 NIV**

3. Demons respond to a _____.

   > *Finally, be strong in the Lord and in His mighty power. Put on the full armor of God, so that you can take your stand against the devil's schemes. For our struggle is not against flesh and blood, but against the rulers, against the authorities, against the powers of this dark world and against the spiritual forces of evil in the heavenly realms.*
   > **EPHESIANS 6:10-12 NIV**

   > *...the one who is in you is greater than the one who is in the world.*
   > **1 JOHN 4:4 NIV**

AUTHORITY

1. The highest authority is _____

    The seventy-two returned with joy and said, "Lord, even the demons submit to us in your name." He replied, "I saw Satan fall like lightning from heaven. I have given you authority to trample on snakes and scorpions and to overcome all the power of the enemy; nothing will harm you."
    LUKE 10:17-19 NIV

    That at the name of Jesus every knee should bow, in heaven and on earth and under the earth.
    PHILIPPIANS 2:10 NIV

2. The authority of _____

    Matthew 4 and Luke 4… "It is written…"

3. The authority of the _____

    They triumphed over him by the blood of the Lamb and by the word of their testimony…
    REVELATION 12:11 NIV

Three Daily Steps

Jesus called his twelve disciples to Him and gave them authority to drive out impure spirits and to heal every disease and sickness.
MATTHEW 10:1 NIV

No, in all these things we are more than conquerors through Him who loved us. For I am convinced that neither death nor life, neither angels nor demons…will be able to separate us from the love of God that is in Christ Jesus our Lord.
ROMANS 8:37-39 NIV

1. Submit yourself _____.

   Submit yourselves, then, to God. Resist the devil, and he will flee from you. Come near to God and he will come near to you. Wash your hands, you sinners, and purify your hearts, you double-minded.
   JAMES 4:7-8 NIV

2. Close any _____.

   Anyone you forgive, I also forgive. And what I have forgiven—if there was anything to forgive—I have forgiven in the sight of Christ for your sake, in order that satan might not outwit us. For we are not unaware of his schemes.
   2 CORINTHIANS 2:10-11 NIV

   "In your anger do not sin": Do not let the sun go down while you are still angry, and do not give the devil a foothold.
   EPHESIANS 4:26-27 NIV

3. Confront your _____.

For though we live in the world, we do not wage war as the world does. The weapons we fight with are not the weapons of the world. On the contrary, they have divine power to demolish strongholds. We demolish arguments and every pretension that sets itself up against the knowledge of God, and we take captive every thought to make it obedient to Christ.
2 CORINTHIANS 10:3-5 NIV

View Freedom videos at freedom.churchofthehighlands.com/media

Journal

WEEK ELEVEN
VESSELS OF HONOR

"In a wealthy home some utensils are made of gold and silver, and some are made of wood and clay. The expensive utensils are used for special occasions, and the cheap ones are for everyday use. If you keep yourself pure, you will be a special utensil for honorable use. Your life will be clean, and you will be ready for the Master to use you for every good work."

2 TIMOTHY 2:20-21

In this passage, the Apostle Paul uses household items as an analogy to describe believers and our ability to be useful to God by serving Him and fulfilling our respective destinies. We see that some items are inexpensive and ordinary, but others are honorable, used for special occasions. In the Master's hand, these are utensils that accomplish great things. Every person is at a different place in his or her walk with Christ. No two stories are the same, and no one starts out as silver or gold; it is a process. If you're unsatisfied with where you are in the process, God is eager to take you to the next level. He is the One who prepares us, refines us, and makes us honorable. Though you may not feel very special or honorable at this moment, God sees you this way. You are not defined or limited by your past. He says in His Word that He makes all things brand new (2 Corinthians 5:17) and He wants to help you become a vessel of honor.

Write Revelation 21:5

Ask Yourself: Am I satisfied with where I am with God? How do I want my life to be different?

At times, we may look at another person and assume from outward appearances that their spiritual walk is strong. While they may appear holy and righteous, looks can be deceiving. We can't tell from the outside what is going on inside a person's heart. It's similar to looking at dishes in a dishwasher—sometimes you can't tell if they have been washed. Even if you inspect them closely and they look clean, they may still be covered in germs. You wouldn't want to eat on a plate that is dirty, no matter how clean it looks on the surface! The Holy Spirit knows when there is something in our lives keeping us from being fit for His use, and He will convict us of sin. Will you let Him reveal those areas to you? He wants to bring you to a new level of personal integrity, and He will do a miracle in your life if you will allow Him.

What areas of your life might need to be confronted and cleaned up by the Holy Spirit? Write them out below as a way of surrendering them to the Lord.

....

....

When we talked about Spiritual Order in Week Four, we discussed justification and sanctification. Remember, justification is an event that takes place when we are saved. When Jesus becomes our Savior, at that very moment, every sin of our past is wiped clean. God removes the junk of yesterday, just as if we had never sinned.

Sanctification, however, is not an event—it's a process. It's a journey through which God molds and transforms our character. As He sanctifies us, God takes us to new stages of faith, continually making us more like Him. He sets us free from habitual sin, purifies our hearts, and empowers us to fulfill the Kingdom purpose for which He created us.

Read the four Stages listed below and identify where you are right now.

Four Stages of Christianity

1. Unbelievers become believers.
2. Believers become disciples who begin to grow.
3. Disciples become leaders who find their purpose in life.
4. Leaders become servants.

It may surprise you to discover that the highest level of our journey as Christians is servanthood. This concept is very counterintuitive to the world's way of thinking. But our greatest goal as Christians is to fulfill the purpose for which God created us, and that requires us to become His servants. Let's look again at 2 Timothy 2:21: "If you keep yourself pure, you will be a special utensil for honorable use. Your life will be clean, and you will be ready for the Master to use you for every good work." Here, the word "Master" is the Greek word "despotes," which refers to a person who is a ruler with absolute power and authority over others. We often think of God as a Friend, a Savior, a Protector, and He is those things—but He is also Lord. That means He calls the shots! And we are called to serve at the pleasure of our King.

Write *Matthew 20:26*

....

....

HONOR IN ACTION

There are three steps we can take to become vessels of honor: offer our bodies, renew our minds, and surrender our wills.

1. **Offer our bodies.**

   "And so, dear brothers and sisters, I plead with you to give your bodies to God because of all He has done for you. Let them be a living and holy sacrifice—the kind He will find acceptable. This is truly the way to worship Him."
   ROMANS 12:1

The body is the place where sin functions. We might sin by saying something with our mouths, looking at something with our eyes, or touching something with our hands. In Job 31:1, a righteous man says, "I made a covenant with my eyes not to look with lust at a young woman." When we are intentional with our bodies, we are able to make conscious decisions to avoid sin. We will make great progress toward becoming a vessel of honor if we are willing to say each day, "Here I am Lord; clean me up. Take each member of my body and the things I have done and wash me. Take my appetites, my addictions, my habits, my tongue, and my attitudes, and consecrate them."

Underline the first word of each command in the following verse:

> *Run from anything that stimulates youthful lusts. Instead, pursue righteous living, faithfulness, love, and peace. Enjoy the companionship of those who call on the Lord with pure hearts.*
> 2 TIMOTHY 2:22

> *Do not let sin control the way you live; do not give in to sinful desires. Do not let any part of your body become an instrument of evil to serve sin. Instead, give yourselves completely to God, for you were dead, but now you have new life. So use your whole body as an instrument to do what is right for the glory of God. Sin is no longer your master, for you no longer live under the requirements of the law. Instead, you live under the freedom of God's grace.*
> ROMANS 6:12-14

2. Renew our minds.

> *"Don't copy the behavior and customs of this world, but let God transform you into a new person by changing the way you think."*
> ROMANS 12:2

Sin functions in the body, but the mind controls the body. Sin begins in the mind.

> *"For though we live in the world, we do not wage war as the world does. The weapons we fight with are not the weapons of the world. On the contrary, they have divine power to demolish strongholds. We demolish arguments and every pretension that sets itself up against the knowledge of God, and we take captive every thought to make it obedient to Christ."*
>
> 2 CORINTHIANS 10:3-5 NIV

In this passage, we see that spiritual warfare is an essential component of the Christian life. Many Christians love God but have no clue how to fight the enemy. We must become equipped for battle because the devil is scheming to destroy you. (1 Peter 5:8)

One of the ways we fight the enemy is by demolishing "arguments." An argument is an "idea." The enemy's goal is to plant thoughts in your mind that are contrary to God's thoughts. A lot of the ideas we've subscribed to, even about God, are simply wrong because they are contrary to Scripture. Don't listen to the voice of the enemy; listen to the Word of God. For example, if the Bible says, "By His wounds you are healed" (Isaiah 53:5), believe it! Warfare is exchanging the report of the world for the report of the Lord. Peace can reign and rule in ours hearts when we align our thoughts with the truth of God's Word.

Here is the main question when it comes to spiritual warfare: Can the devil get you to believe him? We must take thoughts captive and compare them to what the Bible says is true. Minimize your exposure to the worldly thinking found in music, TV, movies, books, and entertainment, and saturate yourself with the Word of God. When you turn off the programming of the world, the voice of God will become clearer to you.

Renewing our mind by the Word of God requires us to use Scripture to combat the lies of the enemy.

Write the truth from Scripture that will dismantle the enemy's lies

LIE	TRUTH
You are confused.	1 CORINTHIANS 2:16
You are fearful.	2 TIMOTHY 1:7
There is no hope.	JEREMIAH 29:11
You're going to die.	PSALM 118:17
Something bad is going to happen.	PSALM 91:10
God can't hear you.	PSALM 34:17
Nothing will ever change.	ISAIAH 43:18-19

3. Surrender our wills.

> *"Then you will learn to know God's will for you, which is good and pleasing and perfect."*
> **ROMANS 12:2**

The body carries out sin, and the mind controls the body, but the will controls the mind. As we surrender our will to God, His perfect will becomes the motivation of our lives. In Matthew 6, Jesus tells us to pray this way: "Your kingdom come, Your will be done." Instead of coming to God with our agenda, we should approach prayer with this mentality: "Father, I want what You want. Have Your way." Come to Him with a neutral heart. If we are biased toward a specific answer to our prayer, God's voice will be difficult to discern.

Write Luke 22:42

....

....

When we pray like this and surrender our will, we are able to honor God with every part of our lives. In this way, we become honorable and useful to the Lord. He will stir up purpose within us and empower us to fulfill our God-given destiny and expand the Kingdom of Heaven.

PREPARE FOR BATTLE

> *"You are a chosen people. You are royal priests, a holy nation, God's very own possession. As a result, you can show others the goodness of God, for He called you out of the darkness into His wonderful light."*
> 1 PETER 2:9

Being useful in the Kingdom is the greatest honor of our lives, but it comes at a price. When we begin to walk in our purpose, we will get the attention of the enemy. We should anticipate his attacks and take them as a sign of encouragement. We are a threat to his plan to keep the world in darkness. Hold on to this truth: you belong to God, and the enemy cannot change that. No one can snatch you out of God's hand. (John 10:28) But we still need to prepare to go to war with the enemy. We need to study our opponent's tactics. The enemy knows the best way to combat our spiritual growth and Kingdom purpose is to trap us in sin. Satan will try to derail us with temptation, making something that is harmful to us seem extremely appealing. When we are tempted, our character is tested through desires in our soul and body.

> *"And remember, when you are being tempted, do not say, 'God is tempting me.' God is never tempted to do wrong, and He never tempts anyone else."*
> JAMES 1:13

We need to understand that God never tempts us! Satan and his demons are the tempters. Unlike God, Satan cannot be everywhere at the same time. But the Bible says that when he fell from heaven, he took one third of the angels with him (Revelation 12:4). Demons are satan's servants, and he has sent them out on mission to destroy our lives. They are always looking for an opportunity to trap us in temptation. Satan has been tempting mankind since he tempted Eve in the Garden. Even Jesus was tempted by the devil. (Matthew 4:1) Jesus, our High Priest, "understands our weakness, for He faced all of the same testings we do, yet He did not sin." (Hebrews 4:15) And because "He who is in us is greater than he who is in the world," we can stand against temptation. (1 John 4:4 NIV)

Read *James 4:7. What happens when we choose to resist the devil's temptations?*

....

....

Write *1 Corinthians 10:13. What will God do for you when a temptation seems unbearable?*

....

....

Jesus gives us insight into how we can withstand temptation. In the Garden of Gethsemane, before He was arrested and crucified, Jesus told His disciples, "Keep watch and pray, so that you will not give in to temptation. For the spirit is willing, but the body is weak!" (Matthew 26:41) In other words, we need to keep the dialogue going with God. Open communication keeps us safe and aware. Wise parents of teenagers know the value of simply talking to their children. A strong, open relationship between parents and children provides protection.

Can you see the active role you play in your own deliverance from evil? You have the choice and available power to withstand the enemy. You can choose to succumb to satan's pressure and give him a foothold in your life (Ephesians 4:27), or you can submit to God and be empowered to defeat the enemy.

THE BREAKDOWN

For rock climbers, a foothold is the place they step so they can advance up the side of a mountain. For the enemy, it is a base for advancing his destruction of God's plans in our lives. A foothold gives him control over an area of our soul, and we allow him to take hold of it when we give in to temptation. Over time, as we give in over and over to a particular temptation, satan's control in that area will grow. Proverbs 5:22 says, "An evil man is held captive by his own sins; they are ropes that catch and hold him." A foothold can ultimately become a stronghold, or an enemy fortress, in our soul. Strongholds are highly dangerous to our spiritual condition and must be torn down.

Areas of bondage that can become footholds in our lives can look like anger, rage, abuse, lust, alcoholism, drugs, profanity, lying, or many other things. Footholds can get lodged in our souls early in life, particularly if a certain sin was part of our environment. For example, if there was often rage in your home, rage might feel like a natural way for you to respond. Areas of bondage can also be the result of the generational sin of our parents or grandparents. Jesus says in John 8:34, "I tell you the truth, everyone who sins is a slave of sin."

How to Break Out of Bondage

> *"Perhaps God will change those people's hearts, and they will believe the truth. Then they will come to their senses and escape from the devil's trap. For they have been held captive by him to do whatever he wants."*
> 2 TIMOTHY 2:25-26

As Christians, God has given us the power to overcome the attacks of the enemy and areas of oppression in our lives. To be free of bondage, we need to repent of sin and cast off the powers of darkness.

Repentance

Often, people believe that just the admission of sin clears their conscience and frees them from any consequence or responsibility. While admitting a sin is part of repentance, it is not full repentance. Repentance not only means admitting your sin but turning away from the sin and choosing to no longer continue in it. Titus 2:11–12 (NIV) tells us that through God's grace and salvation, we can say "'no' to ungodliness and worldly passions, and live self-controlled, upright and godly lives."

Read *2 Corinthians 7:10. What might be missing in a person who struggles with turning from sin?*

....

....

Read *Romans 2:4. What else leads us to repentance?*

....

....

Write *Romans 13:12.*

....

....

If you find yourself in a cycle of sin, don't give up hope! God desires to help you break the cycle. Ask Him to give you godly sorrow that leads to repentance, and meditate on His goodness and His kindness. And remember, "The Lord directs the steps of the godly. He delights in every detail of their lives. Though they stumble, they will never fall, for the Lord holds them by the hand." (Psalm 37:23-24)

Casting Off Darkness

1 John 1:7 says that if we are repentant, the blood of Jesus cleanses us from all sin. But sometimes people can feel that they aren't forgiven even after they have confessed and repented of a sin many times.

If you are feeling this way, it may be because you need to cast off a demon spirit associated with the sin. Over time, sin will allow the enemy to gain a foothold, which feels like a "hook" lodged in your soul. When you are least prepared, you will experience a tug on that hook that makes you feel unworthy and defeated. Those feelings are lies! Because you have repented of that sin, it is covered by the blood of Jesus, and you need to tell the enemy to get out by casting him off in the name of Jesus and removing the hook. This will destroy the demonic hold in that area and release you to experience the complete peace of God's forgiveness. After the hook is removed, ask the Lord to heal the wound and fill the space with His peace and power.

You don't need to be afraid to do this because God has given you the authority in Christ over sin and any dark spirit. The Holy Spirit is with you, and God promises to never leave or forsake you (Deuteronomy 31:8). Remember "For the weapons of our warfare are not carnal but mighty in God for pulling down strongholds, casting down arguments and every high thing that exalts itself against the knowledge of God, bringing every thought into captivity to the obedience of Christ." (2 Corinthians 10:4-5, NKJV)

Below is a list of common struggles you may need to overcome. Identify the areas where satan may have a foothold in your life, and by using the prayer outline above, pray through prayers of repentance, and renounce any dark power.

*rejection • abuse • self-hatred/unworthiness • depression • pride
unforgiveness • greed • guilt/shame • lust/sexual impurity
control • anger • fear*

The specific example of worthlessness is used to show the application the following prayers.

1. **Confess:** Healing starts with admitting we were wrong. We must first acknowledge that we have believed something that is not true and have agreed with the lies of the enemy.
   Father, I confess that I have believed the lie that I am worthless and unlovable. Please forgive me for not trusting that what Your Word says about me is true.

2. **Repent:** To repent means to change direction. When we repent, we choose to turn around and go the opposite way of our previous path. Stop your agreement with the enemy in its tracks and set your mind on a new course of thinking. If anyone has hurt you by reinforcing these lies in your life, forgive them and release them to the Lord.
   I repent and come out of agreement with the lies of the enemy regarding my worth. I recognize that I am greatly valued and loved by God. Father, I

choose to believe Your Word and what You say about me. I choose to forgive _____ for any way in which they have led me to believe that I am worthless, whether deliberately or inadvertently.

It is important to note that when we confess our sins and reject the enemy's lies, we realign ourselves with God's truth. Armed with confidence in His Word, we can take authority over the enemy and remove the effects of his lies from our lives.

3. **Cast off:** We must refuse to allow the enemy to continue to use destructive words or events against us. With the authority of the Name of Jesus, command the enemy to leave.

    I cast off the lie that I am worthless, and I renounce the spirit of unworthiness. In the Name of Jesus and by the power of the Holy Spirit, I break the curse of unworthiness and all its effects in my life. I declare that the spirit of unworthiness has no place in my life.

4. **Bless:** Once the enemy has been removed, fill the place that he held with truth and promises found in Scripture. Speak life over yourself by declaring an accurate view of how God sees you.

    I declare and choose to believe what the Word of God says in Ephesians 2:10, that I am "God's masterpiece, created anew in Christ Jesus." I release the blessing of value and purpose in my life and declare that I am of great worth to God.

Pray for the Holy Spirit's discernment and guidance. He desires for you to be free!

A LIFE OF HONOR

God created you to be a vessel of honor. This role will require you to fight the enemy and reorder your life. Though it can be challenging and messy at times, the rewards are immeasurable. Obedience brings blessing to your life (Deuteronomy 11:27). In addition, God will use you as a catalyst for peace in your family, joy in your community, and change in your school and place of business.

Though the process of becoming a vessel of honor may seem a bit overwhelming on the whole, you will make great progress by being faithful in the small, day-to-day things. Intentionally set aside time to spend with God every day, and apply Tree of Life perspective to every decision you make. In this way, you will begin to shine a light before men that drives away darkness and fills a lost, broken, and lonely world with great hope.

Journal

WEEK TWELVE
WORSHIP

"For the dead cannot praise You; they cannot raise their voices in praise. Those who go down to the grave can no longer hope in Your faithfulness. Only the living can praise You as I do today. Each generation tells of Your faithfulness to the next."

ISAIAH 38:18-19

By this time in the semester, hopefully you know one thing for certain: God's love for you is real and vast. When we truly embrace the love God has for us, we begin to trust Him, and as our relationship with Him grows, we develop a great love for Him as well. Love for God allows our "religious requirements" to become relational joys. What we once saw as duty has now become devotion. It is our delight to know Him and follow His commands.

An overflow of your relationship with God is worship. Worship is more than singing songs; it is a lifestyle. Worship can be expressed through acts of service, words of praise, and giving, as well as singing, dancing and even shouting. Living this way honors our Savior and produces purity, confidence, and strength in us. Then, something amazing happens: We become warriors in God's Kingdom.

Ask yourself: *Am I living the life of a worshipper?*

....

....

LOVE & WAR

Worship is actually an act of warfare against satan and demonic forces! Our worship puts the devil on the run and increases our ability to fight against powers of darkness in the heavenly realms. Psalm 149:6 says, "Let the praises of God be in their mouths, and a sharp sword in their hands."

When we give God all of our attention, we strip the enemy of any power he has over our souls or our bodies as we enter the safety of God's presence. In His Presence, we are protected from every scheme of the enemy. We become like Jesus, who said that the ruler of this world "has nothing in Me". (John 14:30, NASB)

We are able to come boldly into the presence of God because of the blood of Jesus. Hebrews 9:22 says, "Without the shedding of blood, there is no forgiveness." And without forgiveness for our sins, we cannot enter the presence of God. The blood of Jesus has removed every spot and stain from our lives and made a way for us to "approach God's throne of grace with confidence." (Hebrews 4:16 NIV)

NOTHING BUT THE BLOOD

When Adam and Eve sinned in the Garden of Eden, God said "You will surely die." Obviously, He was referring to spiritual death, because they went on to live very long lives after they were banished from the garden. Remember: sin has consequences. But even though God departed from man's spirit when man sinned, He did not abandon His creation. In response to Adam and Eve's loss of innocence and awareness of their nakedness, He covered them with garments made from animal skins. This was the first blood sacrifice.

Throughout the Old Testament, sins were only forgiven when certain animals were sacrificed. God considered these blood sacrifices to be acts of worship. The blood of the animals would be poured on the horns of the altar that sat at the entrance to the tabernacle (sanctuary). The offering was then taken into the Holy of Holies, a sacred place containing the Ark of the Covenant, which housed the tablets with God's Law written on them (The Ten Commandments). The blood would be put on the mercy seat (lid) of the ark, and when the sacrifice was appropriate and right, the presence of God would fall.

In the Holy of Holies, there was a thick veil that separated the Holy Place from the Holy of Holies (also called the Most Holy Place), where the presence of God dwelled. This veil represented the unapproachability of God to anyone but the high priest. When Jesus gave up His Spirit on the cross, the veil in the temple was torn from top to bottom. Notice that it was not torn from bottom to top. God tore this veil from above because He was moving out of that place. A few weeks later at the feast of the Pentecost, God moved into the hearts of believers.

Truth Unveiled

> *"Suddenly, there was a sound from heaven like the roaring of a mighty windstorm, and it filled the house where they were sitting. Then, what looked like flames or tongues of fire appeared and settled on each of them."*
> ACTS 2:2-3

Write Acts 2:4.

....

....

This incredible experience with the Presence of God described in Acts 2 was made possible by the acceptable sacrifice of the blood of Jesus. Thank God for this new and better way for us to experience Him! "With His own blood—not the blood of goats and calves—[Jesus] entered the Most Holy Place once for all time and secured our redemption forever." (Hebrews 9:12) This redemption includes eternal life with God, healing for our souls and our bodies, and deliverance from all the powers of the enemy.

Read Revelation 12:10–12. *God says that satan, the accuser of the believers, who accuses us before God day and night, is overcome. Write verse 11.*

The blood of Jesus has overcome satan. As believers, we are fighting from victory—not for victory! The veil has already been torn; the victory has already been won; satan is a defeated foe. There is nothing separating us from God's Presence! Now, we can be in an intimate relationship with Him. He has declared and expressed His love for us; we need only to receive that love and learn how to love Him in return.

First Love

God desperately longs to connect with our hearts. In Matthew 15:7–9, Jesus says there are people who honor Him with their words, "but their hearts are far from [Him]. Their worship is a farce." Genuine worship comes from a heart consistently connected with God, and that connection happens in two ways: corporately (at church gatherings with fellow believers) and personally (anytime, anywhere).

Corporate worship is important because our faith increases when we join together with other like-minded believers. Even if we come to church or Small Group distracted and burdened by anxiety, our attitudes can quickly change in a worshipful environment. Personal worship occurs when we take initiative, intentionally adjust our attitudes, and cultivate an atmosphere of praise. Wherever we are, any time of day, we can have the attitude of a worshipper and enjoy the presence of God.

Ask Yourself: *Is my worship coming from a genuine place in my heart? What am I doing to create an atmosphere of praise in my daily life?*

LESSONS FROM A RIVER

Though we desire to have a real relationship with God—one like we have seen in others and heard is available to us—sometimes it just doesn't seem possible. Have you ever tried to read the Bible but find yourself reading the same verses over and over without a breakthrough? Or have you tried to pray, but it feels like your prayers are hitting the ceiling? If so, you may need to evaluate your level of surrender. Do you trust God? He wants your trust as much as He wants your heart, because without your trust, your heart will never be completely His.

We often say, "You are my Lord," but when there's a bump in the road, we grab for the steering wheel. Most Christians get distracted by striving to find the happiest, most pleasurable, most personally preferable way to live, but in order to discover God's will for our lives, we must surrender control. It starts when we say, "My life is not my own. I know I've been bought with a high price, and I am your servant by choice. What would you like me to do, King Jesus?" With that kind of attitude, we will live a far more fulfilling life than we ever could have imagined or obtained on our own.

Read Ezekiel 47:1–12. In this vision, the river symbolizes the presence of God. As we venture forward in our relationship with God, we have a tendency to want to keep our toes on the ground, ensuring our head stays above water and we are in control of our lives. But God is inviting us to trust Him, to go deeper, to experience the fullness of His presence. As we surrender control to God, we will be swept away by His love and freely enjoy our journey with Him. When we see that God is worthy of our trust, we will more easily give up control and live in spiritual order.

Four Levels of Worship

Ankle-Deep:
We can enjoy refreshing in God's presence, but we are in full command. We can splash and play, then choose to walk out of the river with no lasting effects on our lives.

Knee-Deep:
The current of God (His Presence) can be felt, but we maintain control. In knee-deep water, we have a good view of those who've ventured out into deeper waters, and we see that in His Presence there is "fullness of joy," (Psalm 16:11 NASB) but we still find security on the riverbank.

Waist-Deep:
Here, the stream of His presence is strong. We've walked into deeper water, but we fight the current and struggle to keep contact with the bottom. Often the fear of what others think or the fear of losing control will tempt us to go back to the riverbank. It is at this place that we make a crucial decision. Who will be in control: God or us?

The Middle of the River:
This is where we can experience the fullness of God's presence. We stop fighting for control, and instead, we pick our feet up and float, allowing His current to carry us. We go where He goes, and it is good.

Most people want to experience God in ankle-deep, knee-deep, or even waist-deep water, but they want to stay in control. In other words, many want to "do the God thing," but reserve just enough control that God doesn't take them too far. Those who live this way have believed a lie that if they abandoned themselves to His control, He would make them do things they don't want to do. They think He would embarrass them or send them to some faraway place they don't want to be. But the truth is, God has only good things for his kids. You will never come to a place of true worship until you are honestly able to say, "God, have Your way."

God led Ezekiel back to the riverbank, and suddenly, to his surprise, there were many trees growing on both sides of the river, and the river was now teeming with life! Ezekiel 47:9 (NASB) says, "Everything will live where the river goes." The leaves of the trees will not wither, their fruit will not fail, and they will bear fruit every month because of the living waters. The trees represent healing and the fish represent harvest. Wonderful things will happen when we abandon ourselves to God's will and His presence: Souls will be saved, people will be healed, and we will experience the life that is truly life!

Write Proverbs 3:5-6.

WAYS TO BE A TRUE WORSHIPPER

1. Give God your affection.

> *"The eyes of the Lord search the whole earth in order to strengthen those whose hearts are fully committed to Him."*
> **2 CHRONICLES 16:9**

God wants to be in a covenant (devoted, unbreakable) relationship with you that involves much more than singing songs. He wants you to desire and enjoy His presence. Worship Him out of the overflow of your heart because He is worthy of the best you can offer Him. Psalm 84:1–2 is a song of craving to worship God. "How lovely is your dwelling place, O Lord of Heaven's Armies. I long, yes, I faint with longing to enter the courts of the Lord."

Finish this passage by writing out the second half of Psalm 84:2.

....

....

2. Commit to unconditional worship.

True worship means praising God even when we don't feel like it. We must be committed to worshipping Him. It's common for us to take a conditional approach to God, just as we do with sports teams. As long as our team is winning and making great plays, we are excited and engaged in the game, but we lose interest and leave early when things don't go as we hoped. In the same way, we praise God when our lives are going well, but disengage and withdraw when things get difficult. The truth is, God is worthy of our worship in good times and bad, when we tangibly feel His presence and when we don't, when we see our prayers answered and when we don't.

The book of Daniel tells the story of Shadrach, Meshach, and Abednego, worshippers of God who were sentenced by King Nebuchadnezzar to be thrown into a fiery furnace for refusing to bow down to other gods. They said, "If we are thrown into the blazing furnace, the God whom we serve is able to save us. He will rescue us from your power, Your Majesty." (Daniel 3:17)

Write Daniel 3:18.

....

....

The quality of our circumstances does not dictate God's worthiness of worship. We must make a commitment that whatever comes in our lives, we will continue to posture ourselves to worship God.

3. Include God in your daily life.

> *"I am the vine; you are the branches. Those who remain in me, and I in them, will produce much fruit. For apart from me you can do nothing."*
> JOHN 15:5

Many of us struggle in our relationship with God because our Sundays do not look like our Mondays. When our everyday world looks different than our "church world" we compartmentalize our lives and limit God's access to our hearts. Our secular and sacred worlds should look the same, equally reflecting the commitment we have made to worship Jesus.

Often, we don't know how to include God in our marriage, parenting, jobs, vacations, or hobbies. What would happen if we made God a part of every area of our lives? When you approach a new disciplinary challenge as a parent, ask God what you should do. When you have difficulty with someone at work, pray for wisdom to handle the situation well. When you have a headache, ask Him to heal you! Don't compartmentalize; God wants access to every aspect of your life. He cares about you and what happens to you. (1 Peter 5:7) Including God in all areas of our lives reveals our level of surrender to Him. As we invite Him to be a part of everything we do, we will have moments of worship every day.

Write Romans 12:1-2 in The Message translation (MSG).

4. Be obedient.

The first place where worship is mentioned in the Bible is a story that reveals a heart of unconditional love for God: the story of Abraham laying Isaac on the altar in Genesis 22. Abraham trusted God with his greatest treasure—his son. And God called this worship.

> *"Therefore, let us offer through Jesus a continual sacrifice of praise to God, proclaiming our allegiance to His name."*
> **HEBREWS 13:15**

Write Hebrews 13:16.

The greatest sacrifice we can give to God is a heart of humility willing to serve Him with unconditional obedience. This kind of worship moves the heart of God toward us. Read this incredible promise from Jesus out loud:

> "The person who has My commands and keeps them is the one who [really] loves Me; and whoever [really] loves Me will be loved by My Father, and I will love him and reveal Myself to him [I will make Myself real to him]."
> **JOHN 14:21 AMP**

5. Show reverence.

> "The fear of the Lord is the beginning of wisdom; all who follow His precepts have good understanding. To Him belongs eternal praise."
> **PSALM 111:10 NIV**

In this verse, "fear" means respect. Our God is like no other—almighty, awesome, and beyond comprehension. It is only appropriate that we approach Him with awe and reverence. True worship requires that we fear the Lord.

> "But the time is coming—indeed it's here now—when true worshippers will worship the Father in spirit and in truth. The Father is looking for those who will worship Him that way."
> **JOHN 4:23**

The Greek word for "worship" in this verse is *proskuneo*, which literally means "to kiss the master's hand in reverence." It indicates both love and respect. This is a powerful combination. When we both fear God, and love Him, we feel safe in the shelter of His immense greatness. This reverent approach to worship allows us to enjoy resting in His presence, and if He tells us to jump, we say, "How high, Lord?"

IN SPIRIT AND TRUTH

> *"Here now is my final conclusion: Fear God and obey His commands, for this is everyone's duty. God will judge us for everything we do, including every secret thing, whether good or bad."*
> ECCLESIASTES 12:13-14

Each day, we have the opportunity to love God and live for Him by aligning our lives with the truth of His Word. We cannot separate our love for God from our submission to Him. God says He wants us to worship Him not only in spirit, with enthusiasm, gratitude, and affection, but also in truth. Worshipping in "truth" requires us to examine our lives and rid ourselves of anything that does not line up with His Word.

We need to ask God to purify us. True worship comes from a place of purity. We can't expect God to be pleased by our jumping and clapping and singing if we do not allow Him to deal with our secret sin and areas where we have fallen short. Hear the heart of humility in this prayer:

> *"Search me, O God, and know my heart; test me and know my anxious thoughts. Point out anything in me that offends You, and lead me along the path of everlasting life."*
> PSALM 139:23-24

Ask the Holy Spirit to reveal anything in you that has grieved Him or reduced His presence in your life, and be willing to confront that area and align yourself with the truth of God's Word. As you go through this process, know this: The voice of the Holy Spirit convicts, but the voice of the devil condemns. You need to discern which voice you hear so that you can respond correctly. Condemnation says, "Here's the problem. Look at it. It's all your fault, and there's no way out." That is not the voice of God. Our Heavenly Father tells us there is no condemnation for those who belong to Christ Jesus. (Romans 8:1) He sent His Son to save you, not condemn you. (John 3:17 NIV) Conviction through the Holy Spirit says, "Here's the problem, but let's do something about it. There is hope and a way out."

Remember the blood of Jesus. In Isaiah 1:18, God says, "Though your sins are like scarlet, I will make them white as snow." Jesus has made it possible for us to walk in purity! Let's make every effort to worship Him with clean hands and pure hearts.

THE MIDNIGHT HOUR

When we are totally focused on God—His goodness, provision, healing, deliverance, holiness—we are actually in a posture of warfare against the enemy. Worship has the power to tear down strongholds and change our environments.

Worship not only brings freedom in our own lives, but it also has the power to set others free. In Acts 16:23–34, we find Paul and Silas in jail. They have been arrested and flogged and are now in the depths of a prison. Chained, weary, and surrounded by darkness, with every reason to be afraid, what do they do? They worship.

> *"Around midnight Paul and Silas were praying and singing hymns to God, and the other prisoners were listening. Suddenly, there was a massive earthquake, and the prison was shaken to its foundations. All the doors immediately flew open, and the chains of every prisoner fell off!"*
> ACTS 16:25-26

Salvation came to many that night, including the jailer and his entire family. That is the power of true worship. Chains fall off, and people are set free. When God is the focus of our love and attention, we will see Him do immeasurably more than we can ask or imagine. (Ephesians 3:20) Choose to love Him with your whole life, and nothing will be impossible for you.

PRAYING FOR PURITY

God desires to purify you. If there is an area of sin in your life that you know you need to deal with, ask Him to forgive you. Use the prayer below as a guide.

Father, I'm sorry for offending You and going my own way. I make no excuses for it. I confess my sin right now. (Identify out loud any sin you need to release to God.) I want this sin out of my life, and I choose to turn away from it. Please forgive me, and make me clean. I receive Your forgiveness now. I know You delight to show me mercy. Thank You, Lord, for letting me off the hook. I make the decision to love You and worship You with all my heart. In Jesus' name I pray, Amen.

Journal

APPENDIX

PREPARING FOR THE CONFERENCE

This semester, you have devoted a great deal of time to studying the truth of Scripture and applying it to your life. There have probably been many moments when you discovered that you had believed a lie that was contrary to God's Word and were challenged to renew your mind and embrace that what God says is true. While this semester of spiritual growth may have been difficult or even painful at times, the effort you've put into the journey is worth it!

The Freedom Conference is the culmination of everything you have studied and discovered over the last 12 weeks, and you do not want to miss it. Each week of study has been thoughtfully designed to prepare you to have a powerful encounter with God.

There are three specific ways you can prepare your heart to receive everything the Holy Spirit has for you at the conference:

1. **Be expectant.**

In your prayer time before the conference, confess to the Lord that you believe He can do anything. Allow Him to fill you with anticipation and hope that He will do the miraculous in your life.

> *I pray that God, the source of hope, will fill you completely with joy and peace because you trust in him. Then you will overflow with confident hope through the power of the Holy Spirit.*
> ROMANS 15:13

2. **Cultivate an attitude of worship and praise.**

Intentionally set aside time every day to worship the Lord. Challenge yourself to go to deeper levels of worship, spending time in His presence, growing in confidence that He is eager to do something powerful for your benefit, and thanking Him in advance.

> *Come, let us worship and bow down. Let us kneel before the Lord our maker.*
> PSALM 95:6

> *For the Lord your God is living among you. He is a mighty savior. He will take delight in you with gladness. With His love, He will calm all your fears. He will rejoice over you with joyful songs.*
> ZEPHANIAH 3:17

3. Shut out the world.

In the days leading up to the conference, limit your exposure to secular influences like television, news, social media, etc. Spend your free time in prayer, worship, and reading the Bible, tuning into the voice of God as you tune out the voice of the world. This will allow your spirit to become sensitive to the leading of the Holy Spirit.

> *Come close to God, and God will come close to you.*
> **JAMES 4:8**

> *Be strong, and do not fear, for your God is coming to destroy your enemies. He is coming to save you. And when he comes, he will open the eyes of the blind and unplug the ears of the deaf. The lame will leap like a deer, and those who cannot speak will sing for joy! Springs will gush forth in the wilderness, and streams will water the wasteland.*
> **ISAIAH 35:4-6**

Make the conference a priority in your schedule. The Lord has been arranging appointments for you throughout your life and this semester and conference are part of His plans! You can expect resistance from the enemy this week, but focus on all that you have learned and set your mind to finish strong!

FREEDOM SONG:
SCRIPTURES FOR LIVING IN FREEDOM

The secret to staying free lies within the Word. The Scriptures are living and active, and they will show you how to live in the Tree of Life every single day as they strengthen your spirit. In dark times, the Word will illuminate your path; in trials, It will bring you peace.

Ask the Lord to inscribe these truths on your heart, and they will become a part of you and all you do. No longer will old ways govern your decisions; instead, you will be transformed into a new creation that radiates the hope of heaven in joy, peace, patience, kindness, goodness, gentleness, faithfulness, and self-control.

How to fight for freedom

It is God who arms me with strength and makes my way perfect.
2 SAMUEL 22:33

"Not by might nor by power, but by My Spirit," says the Lord of hosts.
ZECHARIAH 4:6

For we know that our old self was crucified with Him so that the body of sin might be done away with, that we should no longer be slaves to sin.
ROMANS 6:6

For sin shall not be your master, because you are not under law, but under grace.
ROMANS 6:14

Now the Lord is the Spirit, and where the Spirit of the Lord is, there is freedom. And we, who with unveiled faces all reflect the Lord's glory, are being transformed into His likeness with ever-increasing glory, which comes from the Lord, who is the Spirit.
2 CORINTHIANS 3:17-18

I have been crucified with Christ and I no longer live, but Christ lives in me. The life I live in the body, I live by faith in the Son of God, who loved me and gave himself for me.
GALATIANS 2:20

It is for freedom that Christ has set us free. Stand firm, then, and do not let yourselves be burdened again by a yoke of slavery.
GALATIANS 5:1

Those who belong to Christ Jesus have crucified the sinful nature with its passions and desires.
GALATIANS 5:24

Therefore put on the full armor of God, so that when the day of evil comes, you may be able to stand your ground, and after you have done everything, to stand.
EPHESIANS 6:13

I can do all things through Christ who strengthens me.
PHILIPPIANS 4:13

When you struggle with authority

Everyone must submit himself to the governing authorities, for there is no authority except that which God has established. The authorities that exist have been established by God.
ROMANS 13:1

Obey your leaders and submit to their authority. They keep watch over you as men who must give an account. Obey them so that their work will be a joy, not a burden, for that would be of no advantage to you.
HEBREWS 13:17

Submit yourselves for the Lord's sake to every authority instituted among men: whether to the king, as the supreme authority.
1 PETER 2:13

God is with you

The Lord replied, "My Presence will go with you, and I will give you rest."
EXODUS 33:14

God is our refuge and strength, an ever-present help in trouble.
PSALM 46:1

But now, thus says the Lord, your Creator, "Do not fear, for I have redeemed you; I have called you by name; you are Mine! When you pass through the waters, I will be with you; and through the rivers, they will not overflow you when you walk through the fire, you will not be scorched, nor will the flame burn you. Do not fear, for I am with you; I will bring your offspring from the east, and gather you from the west."
ISAIAH 43:1-2, 5

Never will I leave you; never will I forsake you.
HEBREWS 13:5

When you struggle with pride or surrender

Anyone who does not take his cross and follow me is not worthy of me.
MATTHEW 10:38

Whoever finds his life will lose it, and whoever loses his life for my sake will find it.
MATTHEW 10:39

Therefore, whoever humbles himself like this child is the greatest in the kingdom of heaven.
MATTHEW 18:4

For whoever exalts himself will be humbled, and whoever humbles himself will be exalted.
MATTHEW 23:12

I have been crucified with Christ; it is no longer I who live, but Christ lives in me; and the life which I now live in the flesh I live by faith in the Son of God, who loved me and gave Himself for me.
GALATIANS 2:20

Do nothing out of selfish ambition or vain conceit, but in humility consider others better than yourselves.
PHILIPPIANS 2:3

All of you, clothe yourselves with humility toward one another. Humble yourselves, therefore, under God's mighty hand, that he may lift you up in due time.
1 PETER 5:5-6

Make it your ambition to lead a quiet life, to mind your own business and to work with your hands, just as we told you, so that your daily life may win the respect of outsiders and so that you will not be dependent on anybody.
1 THESSALONIANS 4:11-12

For where you have envy and selfish ambition, there you find disorder and every evil practice.
JAMES 3:16

When anger arises

Be angry, and do not sin; ponder in your own hearts on your beds, and be silent.
PSALM 4:4

A wise man fears the Lord and shuns evil, but a fool is hotheaded and reckless.
PROVERBS 14:16

A patient man has great understanding, but a quick-tempered man displays folly.
PROVERBS 14:29

A fool gives full vent to his anger, but a wise man keeps himself under control.
PROVERBS 29:11

Refrain from anger and turn from wrath; do not fret—it leads only to evil.
PSALM 37:8

The Lord is gracious and compassionate, slow to anger and rich in love. The Lord is good to all; he has compassion on all he has made.
PSALM 145:8-9

And the peace of God, which surpasses all understanding, will guard your hearts and your minds in Christ Jesus.
PHILIPPIANS 4:7

For I will be merciful toward their iniquities, and I will remember their sins no more.
HEBREWS 8:12

When you feel rejected

Though my father and mother forsake me, the Lord will receive me.
PSALM 27:10

I praise you because I am fearfully and wonderfully made; your works are wonderful, I know that full well.
PSALM 139:14

"I took you from the ends of the earth, from its farthest corners I called you. I said, 'You are my servant. I have chosen you and have not rejected you.'"
ISAIAH 41:9

"No weapon forged against you will prevail, and you will refute every tongue that accuses you. This is the heritage of the servants of the Lord, and this is their vindication from me," declares the Lord.
ISAIAH 54:17

So if the Son sets you free, you will be free indeed.
JOHN 8:36

If God is for us, who can be against us?
ROMANS 8:31

In all these things we are more than conquerors through Him who loved us.
ROMANS 8:37

Therefore, if anyone is in Christ, he is a new creation; the old has gone, the new has come!
2 CORINTHIANS 5:17

For we are God's workmanship, created in Christ Jesus to do good works, which God prepared in advance for us to do.
EPHESIANS 2:10

For He chose us in Him before the creation of the world to be holy and blameless in His sight.
EPHESIANS 1:4

When you struggle with purity

Create in me a pure heart, O God, and renew a steadfast spirit within me.
PSALM 51:10

How can a young man keep his way pure? By living according to your word.
PSALM 119:9

Above all else, guard your heart, for it is the wellspring of life.
PROVERBS 4:23

Blessed are the pure in heart, for they will see God.
MATTHEW 5:8

Do not conform any longer to the pattern of this world, but be transformed by the renewing of your mind. Then you will be able to test and approve what God's will is—His good, pleasing and perfect will.
ROMANS 12:2

We demolish arguments and every pretension that sets itself up against the knowledge of God, and we take captive every thought to make it obedient to Christ.
2 CORINTHIANS 10:5

Since we have these promises, dear friends, let us purify ourselves from everything that contaminates body and spirit, perfecting holiness out of reverence for God.
2 CORINTHIANS 7:1

Finally, brothers, whatever is true, whatever is noble, whatever is right, whatever is pure, whatever is lovely, whatever is admirable—if anything is excellent or praiseworthy—think about such things.
PHILIPPIANS 4:8

How much more, then, will the blood of Christ, who through the eternal Spirit offered himself unblemished to God, cleanse our consciences from acts that lead to death, so that we may serve the living God!
HEBREWS 9:14

Let us draw near to God with a sincere heart in full assurance of faith, having our hearts sprinkled to cleanse us from a guilty conscience and having our bodies washed with pure water.
HEBREWS 10:22

When you feel ashamed

Count yourself lucky, how happy you must be—you get a fresh start, your slate's wiped clean.
PSALM 32:1

He does not treat us as our sins deserve or repay us according to our iniquities.
PSALM 103:10

As far as the east is from the west, so far has he removed our transgressions from us.
PSALM 103:12

You are already clean because of the word I have spoken to you.
JOHN 15:3

For He chose us in him before the creation of the world to be holy and blameless in His sight. In love He predestined us to be adopted as his sons through Jesus Christ, in accordance with his pleasure and will—to the praise of his glorious grace, which he has freely given us in the One he loves. In Him we have redemption through his blood, the forgiveness of sins, in accordance with the riches of God's grace.
EPHESIANS 1:4-7

For I will forgive their wickedness and will remember their sins no more.
HEBREWS 8:12

If we confess our sins, He is faithful and just and will forgive us our sins and purify us from all unrighteousness.
1 JOHN 1:9

If anybody does sin, we have one who speaks to the Father in our defense—Jesus Christ, the Righteous One.
1 JOHN 2:1

When you face temptation

I will set before my eyes no vile thing.
PSALM 101:3

Watch and pray so that you will not fall into temptation. The spirit is willing, but the body is weak.
MATTHEW 26:41

Rather, clothe yourselves with the Lord Jesus Christ, and do not think about how to gratify the desires of the sinful nature.
ROMANS 13:14

No temptation has seized you except what is common to man. And God is faithful; He will not let you be tempted beyond what you can bear. But when you are tempted, He will also provide a way out so that you can stand up under it.
1 CORINTHIANS 10:13

But I discipline my body and bring it into subjection, lest, when I have preached to others, I myself should become disqualified.
1 CORINTHIANS 9:27

All of us also lived among them at one time, gratifying the cravings of our sinful nature and following its desires and thoughts. Like the rest, we were by nature objects of wrath. But because of his great love for us, God, who is rich in mercy, made us alive with Christ even when we were dead in transgressions—it is by grace you have been saved. And God raised us up with Christ and seated us with him in the heavenly realms in Christ Jesus.
EPHESIANS 2:2-6

Flee also youthful lusts; but pursue righteousness, faith, love, peace with those who call on the Lord out of a pure heart.
2 TIMOTHY 2:22

For the grace of God that brings salvation has appeared to all men. It teaches us to say "No" to ungodliness and worldly passions, and to live self-controlled, upright and godly lives in this present age, while we wait for the blessed hope—the glorious appearing of our great God and Savior, Jesus Christ, who gave Himself for us to redeem us from all wickedness and to purify for Himself a people that are His very own, eager to do what is good.
TITUS 2:11-14

Submit yourselves, then, to God. Resist the devil, and he will flee from you.
JAMES 4:7

When you feel condemned

They looked to Him and were radiant; their faces were not ashamed.
PSALM 34:5

Do not be afraid, you will not suffer shame. Do not fear disgrace; you will not be humiliated; you will forget the shame of your youth.
ISAIAH 54:4

Instead of your shame you shall have double honor.
ISAIAH 61:7

For God did not send his Son into the world to condemn the world, but to save the world through Him.
JOHN 3:17

But Jesus bent down and started to write on the ground with his finger. When they kept on questioning him, He straightened up and said to them, "If any one of you is without sin, let him be the first to throw a stone at her . . ." Jesus straightened up and asked her, "Woman, where are they? Has no one condemned you?" "No one, sir," she said. "Then neither do I condemn you," Jesus declared. "Go now and leave your life of sin."
JOHN 8:7, 10-11

When he [satan] lies, he speaks his native language, for he is a liar and the father of lies.
JOHN 8:44

Therefore, there is now no condemnation for those who are in Christ Jesus.
ROMANS 8:1

For the accuser of our brothers [satan], who accuses them before our God day and night, has been hurled down.
REVELATION 12:10

When you have been wronged

Love prospers when a fault is forgiven, but dwelling on it separates close friends.
PROVERBS 17:9

But I say to you, love your enemies, bless those who curse you, do good to those who hate you, and pray for those who spitefully use you and persecute you.
MATTHEW 5:44

For if you forgive others for their transgressions, your heavenly Father will also forgive you.
MATTHEW 6:14

Therefore I tell you, whatever you ask for in prayer, believe that you have received it, and it will be yours. And when you stand praying, if you hold anything against anyone, forgive him, so that your Father in heaven may forgive you your sins.
MARK 11:24–26

Do not repay anyone evil for evil. Be careful to do what is right in the eyes of everybody. If it is possible, as far as it depends on you, live at peace with everyone.
ROMANS 12:17-18

Be kind and compassionate to one another, forgiving each other, just as in Christ God forgave you.
EPHESIANS 4:32

See to it that no one misses the grace of God and that no bitter root grows up to cause trouble and defile many.
HEBREWS 12:15

Do not repay evil with evil or insult with insult, but with blessing, because to this you were called so that you may inherit a blessing.
1 PETER 3:9

When your heart is broken

I am the Lord, who heals you.
EXODUS 15:26

He is near to those who have a broken heart and saves those who are crushed in spirit.
PSALM 34:18-19

He heals the brokenhearted and binds up their wounds.
PSALM 147:3

The Spirit of the Sovereign Lord is on me, because the Lord has anointed me to preach good news to the poor. He has sent me to bind up the brokenhearted, to proclaim freedom for the captives and release from darkness for the prisoners.
ISAIAH 61:1-3

Come to me, all you who are weary and burdened, and I will give you rest. Take my yoke upon you and learn from me, for I am gentle and humble in heart, and you will find rest for your souls. For my yoke is easy and my burden is light.
MATTHEW 11:28-30

Who shall separate us from the love of Christ? Shall trouble or hardship or persecution or famine or nakedness or danger or sword? ...For I am convinced that neither death nor life, neither angels nor demons, neither the present nor the future, nor any powers, neither height nor depth, nor anything else in all creation, will be able to separate us from the love of God that is in Christ Jesus our Lord.
ROMANS 8:35, 38-39

Moving past the past

Do not call to mind the former things, or ponder things of the past. "Behold, I will do something new, now it will spring forth; will you not be aware of it? I will even make a roadway in the wilderness, rivers in the desert."
ISAIAH 43:18-19

Therefore, if anyone is in Christ, he is a new creation; the old has gone, the new has come!
2 CORINTHIANS 5:17

But one thing I do: forgetting what is behind and straining toward what is ahead, I press on toward the goal to win the prize for which God has called me heavenward in Christ Jesus.
PHILIPPIANS 3:13-14

When you need peace

Peace I leave with you, My peace I give to you; not as the world gives do I give to you. Let not your heart be troubled, neither let it be afraid.
JOHN 14:27

…and the peace of God, which surpasses all understanding, will guard your hearts and minds through Christ Jesus.
PHILIPPIANS 4:7

When you have money issues

The Lord will open the heavens, the storehouse of his bounty, to send rain on your land in season and to bless all the work of your hands. You will lend to many nations but will borrow from none.
DEUTERONOMY 28:12

Yours, O Lord, is the greatness and the power and the glory and the majesty and the splendor, for everything in heaven and earth is Yours. Yours, O Lord, is the kingdom; You are exalted as head over all.
1 CHRONICLES 29:11

If your wealth increases, don't make it the center of your life.
PSALM 62:10

In the beginning you laid the foundations of the earth, and the heavens are the work of your hands. They will perish, but you remain; they will all wear out like a garment. Like clothing you will change them and they will be discarded. But you remain the same, and your years will never end.
PSALM 102:25-27

Such is the fate of all who are greedy for money; it robs them of life.
PROVERBS 1:19

He who sows righteousness reaps a sure reward.
PROVERBS 11:18

Greed brings grief to the whole family.
PROVERBS 15:27

Whoever loves money never has money enough; whoever loves wealth is never satisfied with his income. This too is meaningless.
ECCLESIASTES 5:10

He will be the sure foundation for your times, a rich store of salvation and wisdom and knowledge; the fear of the Lord is the key to this treasure.
ISAIAH 33:6

For behold, I create new heavens and a new earth; and the former shall not be remembered or come to mind.
ISAIAH 65:17

"Bring the whole tithe into the storehouse, that there may be food in my house. Test me in this," says the Lord Almighty, "and see if I will not throw open the floodgates of heaven and pour out so much blessing that you will not have room enough for it. I will prevent pests from devouring your crops, and the vines in your fields will not cast their fruit," says the Lord Almighty. "Then all the nations will call you blessed, for yours will be a delightful land," says the Lord Almighty.
MALACHI 3:10-12

For where your treasure is, there your heart will be also.
MATTHEW 6:21

No one can serve two masters; for either he will hate the one and love the other, or else he will be loyal to the one and despise the other. You cannot serve God and mammon.
MATTHEW 6:24

If you then, being evil, know how to give good gifts to your children, how much more will your Father who is in heaven give good things to those who ask Him.
MATTHEW 7:11

The devil led Him up to a high place and showed Him in an instant all the kingdoms of the world. And he said to Him, "I will give you all their authority and splendor, for it has been given to me, and I can give it to anyone I want to. So if you worship me, it will all be Yours." Jesus answered, "It is written: 'Worship the Lord your God and serve Him only.'"
LUKE 4:5-8

Be merciful, just as your Father is merciful. Do not judge, and you will not be judged. Do not condemn, and you will not be condemned. Forgive, and you will be forgiven. Give, and it will be given to you. A good measure, pressed down, shaken together and running over, will be poured into your lap. For with the measure you use, it will be measured to you.
LUKE 6:36-38

Sell your possessions and give to the poor. Provide purses for yourselves that will not wear out, a treasure in heaven that will not be exhausted, where no thief comes near and no moth destroys.
LUKE 12:33

When you have money issues *(continued)*

So if you have not been trustworthy in handling worldly wealth, who will trust you with true riches?
LUKE 16:11

Then he said to them, "Watch out! Be on your guard against all kinds of greed; a man's life does not consist in the abundance of his possessions."
LUKE 12:15

Remember this: Whoever sows sparingly will also reap sparingly, and whoever sows generously will also reap generously. Each man should give what he has decided in his heart to give, not reluctantly or under compulsion, for God loves a cheerful giver. And God is able to make all grace abound to you, so that in all things at all times, having all that you need, you will abound in every good work.
2 CORINTHIANS 9:6-8

Do not be deceived: God cannot be mocked. A man reaps what he sows.
GALATIANS 6:7

I have learned to be content whatever the circumstances. I know what it is to be in need, and I know what it is to have plenty. I have learned the secret of being content in any and every situation, whether well fed or hungry, whether living in plenty or in want. I can do everything through Him who gives me strength.
PHILIPPIANS 4:11-13

My God shall supply all your need according to His riches in glory by Christ Jesus.
PHILIPPIANS 4:19

Keep your lives free from the love of money and be content with what you have, because God has said, "Never will I leave you; never will I forsake you."
HEBREWS 13:5

Yet true godliness with contentment is itself great wealth.
1 TIMOTHY 6:6

For the love of money is a root of all kinds of evil. Some people, eager for money, have wandered from the faith and pierced themselves with many griefs.
1 TIMOTHY 6:10

Command those who are rich in this present world not to be arrogant nor to put their hope in wealth, which is so uncertain, but to put their hope in God, who richly provides us with everything for our enjoyment.
1 TIMOTHY 6:17

For, as I have often told you before and now say again even with tears, many live as enemies of the cross of Christ. Their destiny is destruction, their god is their stomach, and their glory is in their shame. Their mind is on earthly things. But our citizenship is in heaven. And we eagerly await a Savior from there, the Lord Jesus Christ, who, by the power that enables him to bring everything under his control, will transform our lowly bodies so that they will be like his glorious body.
PHILIPPIANS 3:18-22

When you feel afraid

Do not be afraid. Stand firm and you will see the deliverance the Lord will bring you today.
EXODUS 14:13

The Lord Himself goes before you and will be with you; He will never leave you nor forsake you. Do not be afraid; do not be discouraged.
DEUTERONOMY 31:8

Be strong and courageous. Do not be terrified; do not be discouraged, for the Lord your God will be with you wherever you go. **JOSHUA 1:9**

Even though I walk through the valley of the shadow of death, I will fear no evil, for you are with me; your rod and your staff, they comfort me.
PSALM 23:4

Though an army besieges me, my heart will not fear; though war break out against me, even then will I be confident.
PSALM 27:3

For in the day of trouble He will keep me safe in his dwelling; He will hide me in the shelter of his tabernacle and set me high upon a rock.
PSALM 27:5

You are my hiding place; you preserve me from trouble; you surround me with songs of deliverance.
PSALM 32:7

I sought the Lord, and he answered me; He delivered me from all my fears.
PSALM 34:4

When I am afraid, I will trust in you. In God, whose word I praise, in God I trust; I will not be afraid. What can mortal man do to me?
PSALM 56:3-5

Cast your cares on the Lord and He will sustain you; He will never let the righteous fall.
PSALM 55:22

He who dwells in the shelter of the Most High will rest in the shadow of the Almighty. I will say of the Lord, "He is my refuge and my fortress, my God, in whom I trust."
PSALM 91:1-2

"Because he loves me," says the Lord, "I will rescue him; I will protect him, for he acknowledges My name."
PSALM 91:14

No evil shall befall you, nor shall any plague come near your dwelling; For He shall give His angels charge over you, to keep you in all your ways. In their hands they shall bear you up, lest you dash your foot against a stone.
PSALM 91:10-12

The Lord is on my side; I will not fear. What can man do to me?
PSALM 118:6

The name of the Lord is a strong tower; the righteous run to it and are safe.
PROVERBS 18:10

Behold, God is my salvation, I will trust and not be afraid.
ISAIAH 12:2 ESV

So do not fear, for I am with you; do not be dismayed, for I am your God. I will strengthen you and help you; I will uphold you with my righteous right hand.
ISAIAH 41:10

When you pass through the waters, I will be with you; and through the rivers, they shall not overflow you. When you walk through the fire, you shall not be burned, nor shall the flame scorch you.
ISAIAH 43:2

Do not fear, nor be afraid; have I not told you from that time, and declared it? You are My witnesses. Is there a God besides Me? Indeed there is no other Rock; I know not one.
ISAIAH 44:8

The rain came down, the streams rose, and the winds blew and beat against that house; yet it did not fall, because it had its foundation on the rock.
MATTHEW 7:25

For you did not receive the spirit of bondage again to fear, but you received the Spirit of adoption by whom we cry out, "Abba, Father."
ROMANS 8:15

What, then, shall we say in response to this? If God is for us, who can be against us?
ROMANS 8:31

For God has not given us a spirit of fear, but of power and of love and of a sound mind.
2 TIMOTHY 1:7

There is no fear in love; but perfect love casts out fear, because fear involves torment. But he who fears has not been made perfect in love.
1 JOHN 4:18

When your heart is heavy

He is near to those who have a broken heart and saves those who are crushed in spirit.
PSALM 34:18-19

Delight yourself also in the Lord, and He shall give you the desires of your heart.
PSALM 37:4

I shall not die, but live, and declare the works of the Lord.
PSALM 118:17

How precious to me are your thoughts, O God! How vast is the sum of them! Were I to count them, they would outnumber the grains of sand. When I awake, I am still with you.
PSALM 139:17-18

See, I have engraved you on the palms of my hands.
ISAIAH 49:16

"Though the mountains be shaken and the hills be removed, yet my unfailing love for you will not be shaken nor my covenant of peace be removed," says the Lord, who has compassion on you.
ISAIAH 54:10

For this is what the Lord says: "I will extend peace to her like a river, and the wealth of nations like a flooding stream; you will nurse and be carried on her arm and dandled on her knees. As a mother comforts her child, so will I comfort you; and you will be comforted over Jerusalem."
ISAIAH 66:12-13

Yet this I call to mind and therefore I have hope: Because of the Lord's great love we are not consumed, for His compassions never fail. They are new every morning; great is your faithfulness. I say to myself, "The Lord is my portion; therefore I will wait for Him."
LAMENTATIONS 3:21-24

And surely I am with you always, to the very end of the age.
MATTHEW 28:20

Then Jesus said, "Did I not tell you that if you believed, you would see the glory of God?" So they took away the stone. Then Jesus looked up and said, "Father, I thank you that you have heard me. I knew that you always hear me, but I said this for the benefit of the people standing here, that they may believe that you sent me." When he had said this, Jesus called in a loud voice, "Lazarus, come out!" The dead man came out, his hands and feet wrapped with strips of linen, and a cloth around his face. Jesus said to them, "Take off the grave clothes and let him go."
JOHN 11:40-44

And I pray that you, being rooted and established in love, may have power, together with all the saints, to grasp how wide and long and high and deep is the love of Christ.
EPHESIANS 3:17-18

And the peace of God, which transcends all understanding, will guard your hearts and your minds in Christ Jesus.
PHILIPPIANS 4:7

When you face trials

Do not sorrow, for the joy of the Lord is your strength.
NEHEMIAH 8:10

For His anger is but for a moment, His favor is for life; weeping may endure for a night, but joy comes in the morning.
PSALM 30:5

My tears have been my food day and night, while men say to me all day long, "Where is your God?" Why are you downcast, O my soul? Why so disturbed within me? Put your hope in God, for I will yet praise Him, my Savior and my God.
PSALM 42:3, 5

Restore to me the joy of Your salvation, and uphold me by Your generous Spirit.
PSALM 51:12

Those who sow in tears shall reap in joy.
PSALM 126:5

I consider that our present sufferings are not worth comparing with the glory that will be revealed in us.
ROMANS 8:18

My brethren, count it all joy when you fall into various trials, knowing that the testing of your faith produces patience. But let patience have its perfect work, that you may be perfect and complete, lacking nothing.
JAMES 1:2-3

Reasons to rejoice

You will show me the path of life; in Your presence is fullness of joy; at Your right hand are pleasures forevermore.
PSALM 16:11

This is the day the Lord has made; we will rejoice and be glad in it.
PSALM 118:24

For you shall go out with joy, and be led out with peace; the mountains and the hills shall break forth into singing before you, and all the trees of the field shall clap their hands.
ISAIAH 55:12

Likewise, I say to you, there is joy in the presence of the angels of God over one sinner who repents.
LUKE 15:10

These things I have spoken to you, that My joy may remain in you, and that your joy may be full.
JOHN 15:11

Now may the God of hope fill you with all joy and peace in believing, that you may abound in hope by the power of the Holy Spirit.
ROMANS 15:13

Rejoice in the Lord always. Again I will say, rejoice!
PHILIPPIANS 4:4

THE ARMOR OF GOD

"Put on the full armor of God so that you can take your stand against the devil's schemes. For our struggle is not against flesh and blood, but against the rulers, against the authorities, against the powers of this dark world and against the spiritual forces of evil in the heavenly realms. Therefore put on the full armor of God, so that when the day of evil comes, you may be able to stand your ground, and after you have done everything, to stand."

EPHESIANS 6:11-19

Use this prayer as an outline to help you prepare for each day. First, put on the Armor of God, and then ask the Holy Spirit to give you wisdom, guide your steps, and help you stand and fight against the enemy.

Put on the Armor of God

The Helmet of Salvation
Thank You, Lord, for my salvation. I receive it in a new and fresh way from You and I declare that nothing can separate me now from the love of Christ and the place I shall ever have in Your kingdom.

The Breastplate of Righteousness
And yes, Lord, I wear Your righteousness today against all condemnation and corruption. Fit me with Your holiness and purity—defend me from all assaults against my heart.

The Belt of Truth

Lord, I put on the belt of truth. I choose a lifestyle of honesty and integrity. Show me the truths I so desperately need today. Expose the lies that I am not even aware that I believe.

The Shoes of the Gospel of Peace

I choose to live for the gospel at all times. Show me how I can be a part of what You are doing on the earth. Keep me focused on the path You want me to walk.

The Shield of Faith

Jesus, I lift the confidence that You are good against every lie and every assault of the enemy. You have good in store for me. Nothing is coming today that can overcome me because You are with me.

The Sword of the Spirit

Holy Spirit, show me specifically today the truths of the Word of God that I will need to counter the snares of the enemy. Bring them to mind throughout the day.

Connect with God

Holy Spirit, I agree to walk in step with You in everything—in all prayer as my spirit communes with you throughout the day.

> *And pray in the Spirit on all occasions with all kinds of prayers and requests. With this in mind, be alert and always keep on praying for all the saints.*
> EPHESIANS 6:18

WHO I AM IN CHRIST

I Am Accepted

JOHN 1:12	I am God's child.
JOHN 15:15	I am Christ's friend.
ROMANS 5:1	I have been justified.
1 CORINTHIANS 6:19-20	I have been bought with a price. I belong to God.
1 CORINTHIANS 12:27	I am a member of Christ's body.
EPHESIANS 1:5	I have been adopted as God's child.
EPHESIANS 2:18	I have direct access to God through the Holy Spirit.
COLOSSIANS 1:14	I have been forgiven of all my sins.
COLOSSIANS 2:10	I am complete in Christ.

I Am Safe

ROMANS 8:1-2	I am free forever from condemnation.
ROMANS 8:28	I am assured that all things work together for good.
ROMANS 8:31-34	I am free from any condemning charges against me.
ROMANS 8:35-39	I cannot be separated from the love of God.
PHILIPPIANS 1:6	I am confident that the good work God has begun in me will be completed.
PHILIPPIANS 3:20	I am a citizen of Heaven.
2 TIMOTHY 1:7	I have not been given a spirit of fear, but of power, love, and of self-control.
HEBREWS 4:16	I can find grace and mercy to help in time of need.
1 JOHN 5:18	I am born of God and the evil one cannot touch me.

I Am Important

MATTHEW 5:13-14	I am the salt and light of the earth.
JOHN 15:1, 5	I am a branch of the true Vine, a channel of His life.
JOHN 15:16	I have been chosen and appointed to bear fruit.
ACTS 1:8	I am a personal witness of Christ.
1 CORINTHIANS 3:16	I am God's temple.
EPHESIANS 2:10	I am God's workmanship.
EPHESIANS 3:12	I may approach God with freedom and confidence.
PHILIPPIANS 4:13	I can do all things through Christ who strengthens me.

ANSWER KEY

Week 1

- *Do more* to get to God.
- Receive the fact that Jesus has already *done it*.
- Keep trying to get *God's approval*.
- Receive the fact that He *already loves you*.
- The Tree of the Knowledge of Good and Evil says: *Obey out of duty*.
- The Tree of Life says: *Obey out of delight*.
- Fall in love *with Jesus*.
- Serve God through *relationships* not *rules*.
- Respond to all sin with *life*.
- Guard your *heart* from going back.

Week 2

- Read Genesis 3:1-8 and notice who is doing what. In verses 7 and 8, what did Adam and Eve do?
  Realized they were naked, sewed fig leaves for covering, hid
- Read Genesis 3:9. What did God do?
  He called out, "Where are you?"
- Read James 4:8 and 2 Chronicles 15:2. What do these passages teach us about our relationship with God?
  Come near to God and He'll come near to you. He is with you if you're with Him. Seek Him, and you will find Him.
- According to Colossians 2:3, what do we find hidden in Jesus?
  Treasures of wisdom and knowledge
- Read 1 Kings 3:10-13. How did God respond to Solomon's request? *Granted him wisdom and included riches and honor because God was pleased with his desire for discernment for administering justice*

- Read Genesis 3:22-24. Why were Adam and Eve driven from the Garden of Eden?
  Because they knew good and evil, making them like God
- From Romans 8:38-39, name all the things that cannot separate us from the love of God.
  Life, death, angels, demons, present, future, powers, height, depth, anything in all creation

Week 3

- Read Matthew 5:39-44 and Luke 6:27-36. In these passages, Jesus tells us how to live as a child of God in innocence and freedom. Using the Scriptures as a reference, describe what living in innocence looks like.
  Answers vary – turning the other cheek, loving your neighbor, praying for those who persecute you, giving up rights freely, giving justice and mercy, loving those who don't love you.
- What does Psalm 37:23-24 say happens when the Godly stumble?
  They will never fall, for the Lord holds them by the hand.
- Read Galatians 4:7 and 2 Corinthians 6:18. What does God say about your identity?
  You are no longer a slave, but a son/heir. He is our Father, and we are His sons and daughters.
- Read Matthew 11:28-30 and write out Jesus' response to the heavy burden that comes from trying to keep the law.
  Come to me, and I will give you rest.
- Read Philippians 4:8 and write out a way to renew your mind.
  Answers vary – Think about what is true, noble, right, pure, lovely, admirable, excellent, praiseworthy.

Week 4

- Read 1 Corinthians 2:14 and write why the world cannot accept the things that come from God.

  Answers vary – They seem foolish. The world cannot understand because the things from God are spiritually discerned.

- Write out the verses below and identify which of the three parts of the soul they address.

  Proverbs 2:10 – Mind

  Psalm 119:167 – Will

  Psalm 139:14 – Emotions

- Read 1 Corinthians 6:12 (NIV) and fill in the blanks:

  "I have the right to do anything," you say – but not everything is beneficial. "I have the right to do anything" – but I will not be mastered by anything.

- Read Galatians 5:19-21 and list the works of the soul-led nature.

  Sexual immorality, impurity, debauchery, idolatry, witchcraft, hatred, envy, discord, fits of rage, selfish ambition, drunkenness

- According to Galatians 6:8, what is the result of living a life that gratifies the body? What happens to a person who lives a spirit-led life?

  Body – sows to please sinful nature, reaps destruction

  Spirit-led – sows to please the spirit, reaps eternal life/a harvest

- Read Psalm 91. According to verses 9 and 10, who will receive the benefits of protection and safety?

  Those who make the Most High their dwelling

Week 5
- Four Blockages of the Heart
    1. *Selfishness*
    2. *Bitterness*
    3. *Rejection*
    4. *Evil Thoughts*
- Three Steps to Transforming the Heart
    1. *Invite the Holy Spirit to show me.*
    2. *Invite the Holy Spirit to change me.*
    3. *Invite the Holy Spirit to fill me.*

Week 6
- Read the following verses. What happens when we give money and things the place of priority in our lives?
  Matthew 13:22 – The Word becomes unfruitful.
  Revelation 3:17 – We don't realize we are actually wretched, pitiful, poor, blind, and naked.
  1 Timothy 6:9-10 – We fall into temptation and are trapped by many foolish and harmful desires that plunge us into ruin and destruction.
- Read the following verses: Psalm 62:10, Hebrews 13:5, Luke 12:22-31. Ask the Holy Spirit to show you how these passages apply to your life.
  Answers vary – Do not set your heart on riches, be free from the love of money, be content with what you have, do not worry about your body – what you will eat or what you will wear

Week 7

- Read Matthew 18:21-35. Through this parable, Jesus explains the profound and undeserved forgiveness we receive as believers. What instruction does Jesus give us regarding forgiveness?

  Forgive not 7 times, but 70 x 7, extend the same grace/forgiveness God has offered you.

Week 8

- Read Matthew 12:34-35. What does Jesus say about the relationship between our hearts and what we say?

  Whatever is in your heart determines what you say.
- Read Proverbs 10:19. What happens when we talk too much? What do sensible people do?

  Talking too much leads to sin, sensible people keep their mouths shut.
- Read the following Scriptures and write the instruction given.

  Proverbs 4:24 – Don't use perverse or corrupt words.

  Proverbs 15:1 – Use gentle words.

  Proverbs 16:13 – Use honest and righteous words.

  Proverbs 16:28 – Don't gossip.

Week 9

- Write Luke 1:38 and note Mary's response to the angel's news.
  I am the Lord's servant. May everything you have said about me come true.
- Read Psalm 119:97-100 and list the benefits of meditating on God's Word.
  Meditation makes us wiser than our enemies, gives us more insight than our teachers, and makes us wiser than our elders.
- Read James 1:22. According to this verse, how can we deceive ourselves?
  Merely listening to the Word and not doing what it says

Week 10

- Three Things to Know
  1. Demons are *real*.
  2. Demons want to *destroy you*.
  3. Demons respond to *higher authority*.
- Authority
  1. The highest authority is the *Name of Jesus*
  2. The authority of the *Word*
  3. The authority of the *blood of the cross*
- Three Daily Steps
  1. Submit yourself *to God*.
  2. Close any *open doors*.
  3. Confront your *enemy daily*.

Week 11

- Write the truth from Scripture that will dismantle the enemy's lies:
    - 1 Corinthians 2:16 – *I have understanding because I have the mind of Christ.*
    - 2 Timothy 1:7 – *God has not given me a spirit of fear and timidity, but of power, love, and self-discipline.*
    - Jeremiah 29:11 – *God has good plans for me to give me a future and a hope.*
    - Psalm 118:17 – *I will not die; instead I will live to tell what the Lord has done.*
    - Psalm 91:10 – *No evil will conquer me; no plague will come near my home.*
    - Psalm 34:17 – *The Lord hears me when I call to Him for help. He rescues me from all my troubles.*
    - Isaiah 43:18-19 – *God is doing something new. He is making a pathway through the wilderness and rivers in the dry wasteland.*
- Read James 4:7. What happens when we choose to resist the devil's temptations?
  He will flee from us.
- Write 1 Corinthians 10:13. What will God do for you when a temptation seems unbearable?
  He will provide a way out.
- Read 2 Corinthians 7:10. What might be missing in a person who struggles with turning from sin?
  Godly sorrow
- Read Romans 2:4. What else leads us to repentance?
  God's kindness

Week 12

All answers for Week 12 are found in Scripture.

Made in the USA
Monee, IL
05 September 2023